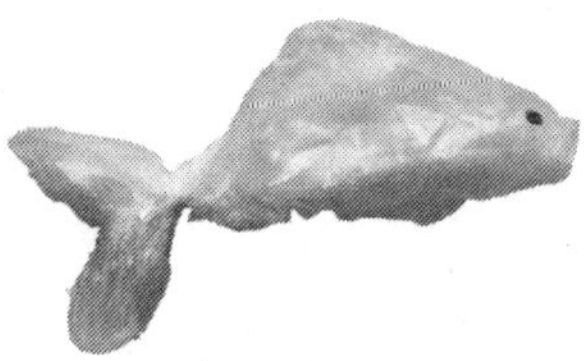

Plastic Free

Celebrating
30 Years of Publishing
in India

"The more time I spend at sea, the more I realise that the solutions start on land. This book will guide you on that journey to making global change for the ocean from your doorstep."

Emily Penn, ocean advocate, skipper, and cofounder of eXXpedition

"Not just an inspiring story and a practical resource, this is evidence that grassroots actions by ordinary individuals and communities can make a material difference to the most wicked of environmental and social problems. Hats off."

Tim Winton, author

"Few people have spent as much time as Rebecca Prince-Ruiz trying to work out how to minimise the plastic in our lives."

Craig Reucassel, comedian and presenter of *War on Waste*

Plastic Free

The inspiring story of a global environmental movement and why it matters

Rebecca Prince-Ruiz
& Joanna Atherfold Finn

HarperCollins *Publishers* India

This English-language reprint edition is a complete reproduction, specially authorized for publication and sale throughout South Asia, published by arrangement with Columbia University Press.

First published in Australia by NewSouth, an imprint of UNSW Press
Published worldwide, excluding Australia, New Zealand, and South Asia, by Columbia University Press

First published in India by
HarperCollins *Publishers* 2023
4th Floor, Tower A, Building No 10, DLF Cyber City,
DLF Phase II, Gurugram, Haryana –122002
www.harpercollins.co.in

2 4 6 8 10 9 7 5 3 1

P-ISBN: 978-93-5629-581-0
E-ISBN: 978-93-5629-582-7

Typeset in 12/16 Adobe Garamond Pro

Printed and bound at
Thomson Press (India) Ltd

MIX
Paper
FSC FSC® C010615

This book is produced from independently certified FSC® paper to ensure responsible forest management.

Contents

To my mothers, Jean and Leigh

– Rebecca

To my parents, David and Vicki

– Joanna

Welcome

'It was billions of micro actions that created the problem and billions of micro actions that can help save it. It all starts with us.'

– Emily Penn, ocean advocate, skipper and co-founder of eXXpedition

This is a book about how ordinary people can make extraordinary changes. It tells the story of Plastic Free July, a social phenomenon involving over 250 million people in 177 countries. Most importantly, it shows how a determined community can become a formidable force.

It started when I asked a simple question: 'I'm going plastic free next month. Who wants to join me?' The small group of people who said yes grew into one of the world's most successful environmental movements.

Some joined because they wanted to avoid their short-lived plastic bags becoming hazardous baggage for the world or because they were worried about where their disposable coffee cup would end up. Others signed up because they had seen wildlife entangled in plastic and want to leave a different legacy for their children. People everywhere are starting to realise the devastating impacts of our throwaway society and the need to contribute to meaningful change.

Plastic Free is the story of all those who have taken up the challenge and changed their own lives and communities, learning from the stumbling blocks and triumphs of others across the globe. You will meet the resilient friends who went from having no retail experience to setting up a bulk food store. You will find out how a photo of a basket of cups inspired cafés all over the world. You will read how one airline removed 30 million single-use plastic items from its operations in one year alone.

Most importantly, this is not just a story about plastic. It is a story of how to make change and invite its momentum into our lives. Whether you are a student, a parent, an educator, a member of a community group, a change-maker, a business operator, a corporate leader or in government, we hope this story will inspire you to join us and others on the journey toward meaningful change. The question for us isn't 'What difference can one person make?' but 'How can we continue to create change together?'

With so many challenges facing our world, there is too much to lose not to try.

1
The day the penny dropped

A day in June 2011 changed everything.

At an unremarkable, gunmetal-grey building on the outskirts of town, the pace was frenetic. A convoy of trucks emptied their loads and kept going back for more. Inside, the mountain grew. Skilled drivers of front-end loaders scooped up massive bucketloads from the floor and fed them onto a conveyor belt to be transported through machinery for processing. The operation was fast and furious – a complex, never-ending, energy-intensive system. Of course, the machines could only do so much. I climbed an industrial staircase and hovered over another scene where the percussive screech was relentless; masked employees in beanies and hi-vis shirts fossicked through the remains of other people's lives. The work was not only tedious but grimy too. A musty haze lingered in the air and settled on my skin. It was more than that, though. I could feel myself sinking under the weight of what I was witnessing.

I had never known this place existed, had never even thought about it, but I was surely a part of it. Here was the end-of-life point of human production and consumerism, and it was driving so much intensity and effort. This was no dystopian horror story, though there were certainly parallels.

It was my local materials recovery facility (MRF for short) – the sorting facility where my household recycling went after it was collected each fortnight from the bin on my footpath. It was where all of my packaging went when I threw it 'away'. Inside, materials were separated out into paper, metal, plastic and glass and sent to be recycled, not just locally but to other states and even other countries.

I trained my focus back onto the workers stooped over the stream of waste. They dragged strips of plastic, used nappies and twisted grocery bags from the conveyor belt and tossed them into skip bins. I even spotted an alarmingly lifelike newborn doll amid the accumulation of trash. The never-ending movement of nimble hands and darting eyes was dizzying. Conspicuous in my hi-vis vest, hard hat and safety glasses, I was overwhelmed and frankly mortified at the amount of rubbish and the role our community had played in it.

I was also deeply unsettled by the work of the staff below me and the unimaginable exhaustion they must have felt. I now understood why the demands of the job stopped many people from being able to endure work at a recycling plant for any length of time. The repetition of pulling foreign items from the chaotic mix of waste strewn along a conveyor belt can lead to a sensation like seasickness. The giddy sensation hit me too, but it was more than that. This was the penny-drop moment when I came face to face with our suburb's waste. With *my* waste.

I realised something that had been teetering around the edge of my consciousness for years. The heart of the problem is how much we consume, and we can't recycle our way out of it.

It was the day that changed everything.

How did I get here?

I'd been learning about the way our actions can affect our environment all my life, but my observations would only come together with hindsight. I spent much of my childhood on a small farm, about half an hour's drive from Boyup Brook in south-west Western Australia. My most enduring memories are of playing in the bush surrounding the farmhouse with my three siblings in a blended family, and of the relative certainty and stability of farm life. My earlier years had been marked by constant change; we had never lived in one spot for long, so the farm gave me a true sense of home.

Our family was quite environmentally conscious even then, though we would never have described ourselves this way; it was just 'what we did'. Living on the farm meant growing and preserving our food, creating things from scratch and making do with what we had. Ducking out to the shops for a missing ingredient or to indulge a whim wasn't an option.

Of course, it wasn't just about my parents' values. We didn't have much money, so some of the decisions were pure thrift. My siblings and I wore secondhand clothes and hand-me-downs. This way of life was also influenced by my dad, who had arrived in Australia as a young refugee from the Spanish Civil War. Dad became a marine engineer and his skills and upbringing reinforced a mindset of using what we had to make what we needed. He was forever fixing things and repurposing objects. He gave me the nickname 'Rebecca Bowerbird' due to my scavenging antics around the farm to find parts for his projects.

Our life on the farm ended abruptly when I was just eight. We were forced to relocate because of rising salinity in the river, which had been caused by overclearing the native bush in the surrounding catchment. My sisters and I were devastated. We didn't want to go and our anger was directed at Dad – this, we believed, was squarely

> 'Being outdoors in the environment is so much a part of my everyday life, when I walk the dog or we go adventuring, it's what we do. I think we take it for granted.'
>
> – Maya, 11 years old

his fault. On the day we left, we reluctantly perched on the farmhouse fence for a photo. I still have that picture. In it, I'm framed by the timber struts, my eyes fixed on the distance. I didn't fully comprehend why we needed to abandon our home, but I think the experience planted those first seeds of environmental awareness. Looking back, it helped me to understand that our actions can have a lasting impact, and the power of childhood experiences.

My teenage years formed new impressions. When I started high school I was quite shy and often felt conspicuous among my peers with my secondhand clothes and homemade lunches. It was a sporty school, which also set me apart. The annual fundraiser involved running laps around the oval and recruiting sponsors to donate. I thought it was a pointless activity and as a slow runner I was keen to avoid it. Thankfully Mum didn't need too much persuading – she said my sister and I could have the day off school. In return, she said, we had to do something worthwhile, so she sponsored us to spend the day walking along the riverbank to pick up litter. At school this was called 'scab duty' and usually meted out as punishment for misbehaviour, but collecting rubbish with my sister was different. We got to spend time together and do something positive. It really felt as though we were making a difference.

Though I may have felt out of my element at school, our street was full of young families that shared tools, helped each other with repairs, enjoyed street dinners and minded each other's children. We were always creative with our time, writing plays, putting on concerts for our obliging parents, publishing our own street newspaper and running cake stalls to raise money for the local animal shelter. It felt great to be part of this innovative tribe of local kids and I have no doubt the experiences fuelled that strong sense of community that I've always been drawn to.

I got an after-school job, and after working for a year at a local grocery store (ironically packing those groceries into plastic bags at the checkout), I pooled my savings and bought a kayak. I spent as much time as I could gliding along the Swan River and observing birdlife, pods of dolphins, the way the water flowed and the boats that ferried in and out of the harbour transporting goods around the world. My dad taught me how to navigate the strong tidal flows and the power of water. *You can't fight the current*, he would say. *You need to go with it and use it to get where you want to go.* It was advice that would guide my way of living in the world.

When I finished school, I didn't have any firm ideas about a career. I guess, like many young people, I just wanted to do something that made a difference, but didn't know what that was. I went with the subjects I'd enjoyed at school and ended up studying botany and geography at university. Despite only scraping through the chemistry and mathematics units, I enjoyed learning about local flora and

> 'We talk about how to bring up our children, avoid waste and live more sustainably while surrounded by all this consumerism. It's really hard and I don't really know how to do it other than by showing them, leading by example, and just having gentle conversations ... I point out rubbish when we see it and when we pick it up it's always the packaging and water bottles – the single-use stuff ... We also go to clean-ups as a family and join in with the community to make a difference. When we make mistakes, we just think maybe next time we can do better.'
>
> – Tracy, Plastic Free July participant

fauna and especially loved going out on field trips and camps and studying a landscape in detail. My curiosity and love of nature deepened, especially in the dry Mediterranean climate of Western Australia where the beauty and biodiversity wasn't always immediately apparent. What became increasingly clear was the connectedness of life, and the way we impact it.

A journey into waste

Understanding the way our actions can maintain or destroy nature's delicate balance took shape once I moved into government and consultancy roles in natural resources management. Over the next two decades, I learned about the challenges of managing our impact on the environment and using resources sustainably. Upstream of my former paddling adventures on the Swan River, an invasion of aquatic weeds that had escaped from a home aquarium choked a long stretch of river. It was a challenge to remove them without further impacting the ecosystem and there wasn't a perfect solution. Using both mechanical and chemical controls we resolved the situation, after careful research, monitoring, and consulting with the local community. I also worked for marine biologist Jeremy Prince and a group of abalone divers surveying populations and creating underwater maps of the stocks in an effort to manage the fishery more sustainably. I discovered that the projects that *really* inspired me were those that involved engaging with local communities where I saw how connected people were to their environment and how much they cared – even though their ideas about the solutions could be wildly different.

This phase of life was also a learning curve in unanticipated ways. The work that Jeremy and I were doing on environmental management with communities grew into a relationship and we were soon juggling the demands of travel and running a consultancy with the arrival of our three children. I took time out to raise our family. Discovering the world through the eyes of our inquisitive and energetic kids kept me occupied, so it was only natural that when our youngest started school in 2008 I felt restless. I enrolled in a local community course called Living Smart where we explored different topics relating to sustainability such as water, energy, transport and waste. I remember thinking I wouldn't need to attend all the sessions because I was already on the right track, but I soon realised there was a lot to learn. The course focused on behaviour change and offered practical solutions that were a natural extension of our family's lifestyle. It felt good to set goals and take small steps each day – such as riding our bikes – which then led to next steps: we put a bike rack in the front yard to save the usual pre-ride untangling, which then encouraged us to ride more frequently. I also started a 'frocks on bikes' group where a group of us would 'frock up' and cycle to our local restaurant – it felt important for cycling to be normal and not just about racing and lycra. Doing the Living Smart course with like-minded people was a positive experience. We all knew that together we were making a difference.

Around the same time, a serendipitous encounter with an old friend led me into a short-term contract as a waste and sustainability educator at the Western Metropolitan Regional Council in Perth. The council operated a waste transfer centre funded by a fee on every tonne of waste delivered through the gate. Part of that fee was used

> 'Ironically the biggest impact we've found from the Living Smart course is around community. It kickstarts a belief in people that they can make a change, then it gets a bunch of like-minded people to go, "That was great" and then those people go on a journey which often leads out into their community.'
>
> – Shani Graham, Living Smart Facilitator

> 'It was a big wake-up call to realise hardly any of the products we were purchasing were being recycled properly, if at all. Then I learned about all the energy it takes to recycle … It just seemed insane. One of the recycling company representatives said if there was a too high level of contamination of general waste in any one load of recycling they collected it could all go to landfill. When I learned all this I thought, "Crikey, I just need to reduce everything."'
>
> – Hamish, Plastic Free July participant

to deliver the Earth Carers education program. As well as educating the community about general sustainability, the core focus of the organisation was to inform people about the services offered at the transfer station – such as electronics (e-waste) recycling, battery recycling and household hazardous waste disposal – as well as ways to manage their waste at home through solutions including composting and worm farms. At the time we talked about the 'Three Rs' of reducing, reusing and recycling, but the core focus was on recycling. A 'do and then learn' philosophy engaged people in creative ways. We would run events such as clothes swaps and fashion shows to highlight ideas around repurposing clothes, or interactive presentations at school assemblies where one of us would dress up as a battery while the other shared information on proper disposal methods and keeping hazardous items out of landfill. Twice a year we ran an intensive Earth Carers course that took people on the journey of their waste. The weeks led to years and to my surprise I became hooked on this strangely compelling waste issue.

The more I delved into resource management and practical solutions, the more my own behaviour changed and I started to focus on what our family could do to make a difference. Until my visit to the materials recovery facility (MRF) in 2011, the fate of our household waste was something I'd not given a lot of thought to. It was such an easy process. Unlike times gone by, we didn't need to deal with our waste in our own backyards through positive means such as composting or keeping chickens, or in less ideal ways such as incinerating or burying it in holes (though in places without modern waste management infrastructure, waste disposal by burning and or dumping in the environment or in unmanaged sites still continues).

Bringing it all together

That day in June 2011 was the day I *really* understood that our waste didn't just go away after the council trucks collected it. 'Away' was in that gunmetal-grey building with its mountains of rubbish. That day I saw the reality of my community's recycling efforts, and I was struck by the challenges of dealing with one 'recyclable' material in particular: plastic.

All the plastic bottles and packaging had the 'recycling' symbol on them, which had made me think that they were okay to use in the first place. But good intentions don't necessarily lead to impressive results: just because a material *can* be recycled, that does not mean that it *will* be recycled. I learned the question we need to ask isn't 'Is it recyclable?' but 'Will it be recycled?'

I was shocked to learn that only 9 per cent of all the plastics ever made have been recycled, and only 0.9 per cent are recycled more than once. The fact is that it's largely easier and cheaper for manufacturers to use virgin plastics rather than recycled material.

The scientist within me was curious to learn more about this plastics problem. What about the plastics that aren't recycled or sent to landfill – where do they end up, how do they get there and what is their impact?

•

When we begin to question the way we have done things in the past, we are usually led there by a significant event or the culmination of several influential experiences. For me, it was a trickle effect that had started with my earliest life experiences: having to leave my home due to human damage to our environment, and the environmentally responsible philosophy instilled in me by my parents. Those experiences led me to study botany and geography; they inspired my curiosity and a sense of responsibility. My close encounters with the Swan River's dynamic tidal changes at the edge of Fremantle Harbour expanded the limits of my knowledge. The discoveries represented a continuous opening out for me, and they fed my desire to learn more. In contrast, the recycling centre conveyor belt, with its enclosed black loop of endlessly rotating rubbish, made me feel as though the world was closing in on me.

My penny-drop moment was devastating, but looking back I can now think of it in a more positive way. I felt the conviction to make change so strongly that day and the importance of taking personal responsibility. With that conviction I started to think about the other choices I could have made in the past and what the future alternatives might be. Filling my recycling bin with packaging no longer felt like it was doing the planet a favour. Sure, it was better than sending those things to landfill, but my own journey into waste made me realise that everything I purchased and used had an impact not only in terms of production, but also in where it would end up. It was an opportunity to make better choices.

In the Earth Carers office, I was surrounded by people who shared a can-do mindset about taking action and tackling problems by making incremental changes to their lives. So, with a fair degree of optimism and a huge dose of good old-fashioned Spanish impulsivity, I voiced the sentence that would change my life, and ultimately the lives of many, in diverse and profound ways. That day in June seemed as good a time as any to make the call.

'I'm going plastic free next month. Who wants to join me?'

2

The challenge begins

It is six in the evening at a local community centre in Cottesloe, a beachside suburb of Perth. Gathered around a blue tarpaulin are harried mums fresh from witching hour, office staff who haven't had time to change out of their nine-to-five suits, retirees ready for some post-dinner action and slouched students taking a well-earned study break. The body language is telling: there are pondering hand-on-chin types, nervous hand-claspers and 'What have I signed up for?' faces hiding in the back row. We are here with an Earth Carers group for what could be best described as 'Waste 101' – a crash course in waste levies, recovery rates and recycling services, and a hands-on waste encounter known as a 'bin audit'.

Regardless of where we live, and whether or not we want to admit it, we all make daily choices that leave behind a waste trail. Waste unites us, though sometimes we can't see that until it is demonstrated in ways that aren't always palatable. The attendees have come of their own free will in lieu of more appealingly titled evening courses like Conversational Italian and Watercolour Techniques.

The bin audit is a get-down-and-dirty ordeal, where a week's worth of general household waste is donated by an anonymous but consenting household, wheeled into the centre of the tarpaulin and upended. This is the real deal – we actually never know what will be in there – plastic meat trays complete with dried chicken blood, mouldy bread, fermenting vegetables, out-of-date cream, soiled nappies and all the other refuse that people accumulate in their general waste bin for others to deal with. The face-your-waste confrontation can be strangely compelling. People stare at the pile in amazement. The stench can be stomach churning and you never quite know what will be exhumed.

Around the edge of the tarpaulin are five signs:

- Reuse (still have another life)
- Donate (still useful and in good condition)
- Organics (could go to compost, worm farm or chickens)
- Recycling (items accepted in household recycling bins)
- Other disposal (specialised recycling or disposal)

We hand out gloves and metal tongs to those brave enough to volunteer and ask them to study each item and consider alternatives to the general waste bin. Once people take on the challenge, they are inventive and thoughtful about the possibilities. Apples with slightly wrinkly skin go into the reuse pile to make stewed apple (though not these ones, of course). A bunch of coathangers is donated to a charity store. Clean glass jars are listed for free on an online

> 'I'd never opened a bin, tipped it out and had to sort and separate it. We have very little ownership of our waste because we are separated from the waste we create. I was already on a journey and understood the statistics about waste, but the bin audit made it very tangible. It gave us a chance to see that we could be part of the solution. If we had that level of accountability for every piece of waste we created we'd be far less wasteful.'
>
> – Darryl, bin audit participant

billboard or 'buy nothing' group for use in jam making. Fruit and vegetable scraps are composted or added to water for homemade stock. Inevitably during this exercise, the participants retrieve items that can be recycled such as newspapers or tins. There are often items such as batteries, garden chemicals and paint that should have been dropped off at a facility for correct disposal, not chucked out in a bin destined for landfill.

As facilitators, we join in on the banter, but we also take a step back and let the group come up with solutions. There is a buzz of conversation and plenty of constructive comments. Some people sort with immense enthusiasm; others are more reticent and happy to watch, adding in creative suggestions. Some are so overpowered by the cloying stench that they have to dash outside for fresh air.

One certain result of this activity is that the pile of what is truly rubbish in the centre of the tarpaulin always gets smaller – usually it is at least halved – as people find alternatives for their waste. The other certainty is the sheer volume of single-use plastic: dirty nappies, plastic bags, takeaway containers, bread bags, multiple layers of plastic from groceries and a miscellany of other plastic items that will never break down, all destined for landfill.

The first Plastic Free July

When I first expressed my impulsive 'I'm going plastic free next month' idea, it was to my Earth Carers colleagues Amy Warne and Nabilla Zayan. Then we pitched the idea to the participants in the Earth Carers course – people from different walks of life who believed in the 'from little things, big things grow' philosophy. Our blueprint for change, in our isolated corner of Australia, was to recognise a problem, transform the way we did things and share those new ideas with our community.

Admittedly, a certain degree of naivety came into play, and perhaps that was a good thing. If we'd thought about it too deeply, or if our team's creativity had been restricted by bureaucratic protocols, perhaps it would never have taken off. Instead, the positive response from this small group of people for a challenge that basically named itself was how the first Plastic Free July came to be.

To be honest, I didn't think a one-month plastic-free challenge would be that difficult. I hadn't accepted a plastic shopping bag for years. I didn't buy bottled water, being far too frugal to buy something I could get for free from the tap. But one of my first challenges was realising that although I was already avoiding plastic shopping bags, I needed to find an alternative for the flimsy plastic produce bags for fruit and vegetables. Going to the checkout with enough groceries to feed a family of five and juggling loose apples and potatoes quickly lost its appeal. It was no doubt quite frustrating for the checkout operators too. I tried the brown-paper mushroom bags as an alternative, knowing that the paper was technically more recyclable. They didn't last, though, and I felt guilty about the trees. I didn't want to simply substitute one single-use item for another. This issue was resolved when I managed to source lightweight netting 'produce bags' made from recycled plastic bottles from a local business called Onya.

July was challenging for other reasons. As the birth month of our very sociable daughter Pepita, there was a mandatory birthday event involving lots of mouths to feed (I vividly remember wishing I had chosen a different month to have this great idea). Still, we managed to take a group of nine hungry fourteen-year-olds away for a birthday gathering and only used two pieces of single-use plastic.

A week-long family camping trip to the remote Pilbara region proved more difficult. At an isolated roadhouse we were presented with plastic-wrapped sandwiches and no alternatives. How had I been going into roadhouses for years and never noticed how much plastic packaging there was? It was as though I was seeing the world through a different lens. My children still remember my frustrated rant when I got back in the car. Going hungry on a 1000-kilometre road trip wasn't an option, so in this case plastic won, but I learned a valuable lesson in how to be more prepared. Baking cookies and buying dried fruit and nuts from the bulk food store for snacks was a win. Thinking of an alternative to packaged rice cakes or wraps was a definite fail – I couldn't find anything else that would last a week in our tent and still be edible. It was a steep learning curve trying to live without single-use plastic, and the fact is that I didn't. But we certainly used a lot less, and that felt great.

The inaugural challenge was simply to change ourselves; our only resources were enthusiasm and the desire to give it a go. I'll admit that we literally made it up as we went along. There was nothing sophisticated about our communications; it was just a few group emails that shared ideas and suggested local sources of plastic-free alternatives, as well as many cups of tea as we chatted and tried to figure things out. There were some guiding principles, though. It was very important that the challenge was achievable, so from the outset we kept our plastic-free mission simple and inclusive. Taking part involved deciding whether to do it alone or with family members, pledging to try to go without single-use plastic, sharing ideas, and keeping any plastic packaging we acquired in a Dilemma Bag. There was quite a bit of discussion on what to name this collection. Initially it was suggested that we call it a Shame Bag, but we settled on the word 'dilemma', which illustrated the spirit of our approach – we focused on the positives, on what people *could* do, rather than what they couldn't avoid. The word dilemma also suggested a problem that could be worked through and, if not solved, at least thought about carefully. There was no shame or blame; there was only discussion and communal problem solving.

It was perhaps fortunate that we were only doing it for ourselves, because the broader sentiment around plastics at this time would

> 'In some ways [my partner and I] were already on the journey because we shopped at a bulk food store. I remember learning how to make my own yoghurt. Despite this, it was definitely an eye-opener and in every part of my life I started to register more and more plastic. There were so many plastics that I had seen before but never really noticed. I'd open a cardboard box and there was a plastic bag inside. When I opened a beer, for the first time I realised there was a plastic lining underneath the metal lid. Doing Plastic Free July made me more aware, but also more diligent about finding alternatives.'
>
> – Nabilla Zayan, colleague and participant in the first plastic-free challenge

have made it difficult to get the message out. This was made clear when I eventually did my very first radio interview. I was keen to share my observations of the recycling facility and what actually happens to our waste, as well as how easy small steps towards reduction could be. In his introduction, the presenter basically told me this was impossible. 'Your phone has plastic, your car has plastic and your computer even has plastic; it's just not possible to go plastic free,' he said. Despite my best efforts to acknowledge that plastic has value and to steer the conversation towards plastic that was single-use and disposable – and 'the stuff we just use for a few minutes' – I was unable to effectively get that concept across.

Plastic waste just wasn't seen as a pressing mainstream issue, and we were no doubt viewed as naive environmentalists wanting to threaten the status quo with our impossible ideas. We forwarded a story highlighting our efforts to the local newspaper, but it mustn't have been deemed newsworthy; there was no interest and it wasn't published. Not to be defeated, we kept on sharing the idea with anyone who would listen, and our network of waste educators and colleagues in local government around the city embraced the concept.

But plastic is everywhere

One thing everyone in the group agreed on was that making changes was initially much harder than we had anticipated. We live in a world where plastic is used every day and in a multitude of ways. It is durable, cheap and convenient, making it an obvious form of packaging; we are quite literally surrounded by it, so trying to eliminate it from our lives was no small challenge. During that first month, I remember going to the supermarket to buy pasta and seeing for the first time that it came packaged in plastic. I honestly think I'd never noticed that before. Every time I tried to shop in a large supermarket I would come out almost empty handed. So we sought out alternatives, and started to shop at farmers' markets and local stores.

> 'When I first started [Plastic Free July] I remember feeling really excited by it, and I found the bags, straws and bottles were the really easy stuff. Then about the two-week mark, I saw things that were really hard to go without. I remember feeling pretty overwhelmed … We didn't take everything away at once that our one-year-old daughter was used to eating – we just did things one by one. I would definitely have spurts of doing 100 per cent plastic free but then I would freak out and burn out. I've become a lot gentler with myself now. I still try my absolute hardest and do as much as I can but will give myself a break occasionally.'
>
> – Emily Ehlers, Plastic Free July participant since 2012 and blogger, *Eco with Em*

START SMALL

1 See what plastics are in your life. Start by looking in your fridge, food cupboard and bin.
2 Decide on one or two items to change and start with them.
3 Share your resolve with a friend or family member.
4 Join the challenge at plasticfreejuly.org, no matter what month it is.

With practice, good habits formed and we became far more consistent in remembering our reusables. Most of us had reusable bags, coffee cups and water bottles, but it was easy to leave them at home or in the car. Having a coffee in a disposable cup was something we had all done without feeling any consequences, but doing the challenge held us accountable (or at least made us feel guilty). It was also heartening to see family members getting in on the act, even if it was only to appease us.

My colleague Amy shared the story of one of her brothers-in-law who went to a football match and knew in advance that the stadium only sold beer in disposable plastic cups. Since a footy game without beer is a bit like a day without sunshine, his game plan was to salvage a suitable one-litre plastic container from his recycling bin. The bar staff had been happy to fill his reclaimed yoghurt containers with cleansing ale and he was chuffed because they were filled to the brim, so he got a bit of extra bang for his buck. The following year, Amy told us how his planning and sophistication had gone up a notch: he replaced his serviceable but unrefined yoghurt containers with a reusable stainless-steel coffee cup.

A strong feeling of unity formed as our group exchanged ideas and recipes as well as more specific solutions. The dilemma of pasta became a lengthy discussion. Someone suggested a brand that came in a cardboard box. Another had found it available in bulk at a local store. A third person volunteered their Italian nonna's family recipe to make pasta but we all had to swear to secrecy. In some ways it was like going back to how things used to be. It was a challenge – frustrating and at times overwhelming – but sharing the journey provided support and a sense of purpose.

Do it first – then learn

Plastic Free July became a tool to enable community-led, organic change to help people make their lives more sustainable. That's really how simple it was. Plastic definitely wasn't the poster child of our waste problem as it is today. As my media encounter had made patently clear, people didn't understand that the problem wasn't necessarily plastic as a material, but the way we were using it just once. We were making a change towards sustainability through reducing our reliance on plastic. A few people making small changes is where a broader culture change begins.

At the same time, we discovered that the 'do and then learn' philosophy – rather than 'learn and then do' – worked for the plastic-free challenge. Our experiences with Earth Carers had already taught us that. I had already known that reducing plastic was important, but doing a challenge on a daily basis offered an evolving structure to implement those changes. For myself, I realised that it was really beneficial to make a commitment and be accountable among a group of like-minded people. It was much easier and far more enjoyable than doing it alone. As a team, we were surprised to realise that the challenge had value for other people too.

On the last day of July 2011, some of that first group of Plastic Free July participants got together for an end-of-challenge debrief. We brought in our Dilemma Bags for a show-and-tell, shared stories of our successes and failures, celebrated our efforts – and everyone got a bamboo toothbrush. While the challenge showed us that we were surrounded by plastic, it also taught us that there were lots of solutions. Convenience foods such as snacks in plastic packaging or in containers featured in many Dilemma Bags; we acknowledged that many of these items weren't that healthy for us. There was also an unexpected amount of plastic packaging we hadn't thought about, such as postal satchels. Someone had purchased a shower fitting that came encased in multiple layers and types of packaging (plastic film, foam peanuts and bubble wrap) – all for an item that didn't require anywhere near that much protection.

It could have been overwhelming but the Earth Carers' motto many of us had previously adopted worked well:

Do it together, focus on the positives, share the solutions and do what we can.

Thank goodness wine comes in glass bottles. Euphoric after a celebratory glass of champagne, we were convinced it was worthwhile and decided we'd do it again.

And we did.

The second Plastic Free July

In Plastic Free July's second year, we drew on what we had learned from the first challenge and started to develop a more coordinated approach. Because it had a name, a defined time frame and focus, it became a platform that people could join and talk to others about.

Often people told us that they had felt alone and disconnected from their family, friends or communities in their concerns about waste. I had felt that way too. I remember the first time I bravely ordered a drink without a plastic straw. It came with two. It was disheartening but sharing this story with others gave me some ideas about asking in a different way, telling people why I was asking, and giving feedback in a constructive way when things did go wrong. It was also surprisingly helpful to have an 'excuse' to be different. To be able to say 'I'm doing Plastic Free July – can you please serve this drink without a straw?' was somehow easier than just asking for no straw. We belonged to something bigger than ourselves and it gave us a purpose. Sustainability educators were always talking about the Three Rs: reduce, reuse, recycle. This was doing something practical to harness that first 'R': reduce.

Getting the message out

Although it had never been our original intention, Plastic Free July was starting to become a popular movement and it felt important to share it further. To spread awareness and harness what the challenge stood for, we realised we needed a logo. Again we kept things 'in the family' and after several design attempts, Plastic Free July participant and local graphic designer Kate Lindsay created our original iconic turtle with its colourful carapace made up of a crossed-out circle of common plastic items. It was the perfect visual for our campaign,

The original Plastic Free July turtle logo,
designed by Kate Lindsay

showing both why and what we were doing. With the participant group expanding, we started a registration process. People were able to formally sign up online, and we sent group members a regular weekly email with ideas and encouragement to share the challenge with others.

We quickly realised that mainstream media was not a vital communications tool because social media had arrived. We started a Facebook page and were euphoric when we reached 100 followers. Our first ever post was a picture of a worn brown-paper bag surrounded by loose vegetables on my kitchen bench. The caption read:

> 'Just bought fresh pasta on my way from work and used a paper bag I had previously bought bread in. The girl smiled and said, "More people should do it!"'

It was at this point that people from all over the world started engaging with the challenge. We were, of course, delighted that our challenge was resonating with people beyond our community. It also allowed us to expand our knowledge base and to learn of some of the single-use plastic issues in other regions in a very personal and proactive way. Having online conversations resulted in diverse problems and responses and language was no barrier since social media offered a visual way to share solutions (as well as failures).

One of the first questions asked on our page was 'How do I line my kitchen bin without a plastic bag?' It was a quick task to pull out from under my kitchen sink the bin that was lined with several pages of the local community newspaper, take a photo and post it to Facebook. Within an hour 2000 people from around the world had seen that photo and it was enthusiastically shared – especially on Vancouver Island in Canada, for some reason. Many people commented that they now thought they could go plastic bag-free. People also shared their creative ideas, including freezing food scraps till bin day if they didn't have a home compost or using other types of packaging to bag their rubbish.

At the time there was hardly any information available to help people go plastic free. One source that helped us a lot in the early days was the blog *Fake Plastic Fish* written by Californian accountant-turned-activist and blogger Beth Terry. She had decided to stop buying new plastic in 2007 after seeing a photo by artist Chris Jordan of a dead seabird filled with plastic. Being an accountant, Beth didn't just avoid plastic; she also collected and tallied every piece of plastic waste she accumulated, which in 2011 amounted to just 2 per cent of the average American's tally. Her blog and later book *Plastic Free: How I kicked the plastic habit and how you can too* became our go-to guide.

Locally, we expanded our activities with a community screening of *Bag It*, a 2010 documentary that explores the effects of plastic through the eyes of one man embarking on a journey to change his habits. The film is a moving call to action, but it also manages to talk about ways to reduce plastic in an accessible way. We screened it at the local school and involved the students in making plastic-free snacks. Local wholefood chef Jude Blereau facilitated a workshop teaching people how to avoid buying processed, packaged foods by making simple and delicious basic food items such as granola and

'I found a great bulk store at the markets and have been getting all my tea, chocolate, grains, sugar, everything from there using bags I sewed. It's been working a treat and our shopping bills have dropped because we've been really planning meals, snacks and treats so we could do a single plastic-free shop each week. It's a huge success in our household.'

– Emma, Plastic Free July participant, 2012

FOOD TIPS

In 2012, wholefood chef and author Jude Blereau wrote a 'Plastic-Free Cooking Tips and Recipes' handout for Plastic Free July, and ran a workshop. Along with recipes, she provided helpful plastic-free food preparation tips:

- Keep a range of bags to put fruit and vegetables, flour and grains in.
- Put leftovers in recycled glass jars, e.g. jam jars.
- Store vegetables in glass Pyrex containers.
- Keep herbs fresh for days by placing a damp cloth in a Pyrex dish with the washed herbs on top. Seal with a lid and keep in the fridge.
- Make as much as you can from scratch to reduce packaging.

savoury crackers. Each week our newsletters shared ideas as well as people's achievements, their success stories and their challenges. As an evolving movement, we continually looked for ways to raise awareness about the problem and help people to find solutions.

The challenge spread to collecting litter during Two Hands Project beach clean-ups every week. The Two Hands Project is a simple but powerful idea that encourages people to clean up their local beach or area for 30 minutes and post a 'trophy photo' on social media showing what they have collected. Two Hands co-founder Paul Sharp is a forensic detective of the plastic world, and he showed us how to identify the items we found. Two identical-looking white plastic sticks, for example, turned out to have different origins – one was a lollypop stick, while the other had three grooves in each end, which indicated it was from a cotton bud. Paul also gave a talk on the global plastic pollution issue, and what he encountered in the open ocean during his sailing expedition in the North Pacific after Japan's earthquake and tsunami in 2011. On the three-week voyage, Paul described seeing floating plastic every few minutes, from polystyrene to beverage bottles, buckets, helmets, crates and plastic fragments. Most surprisingly, on the whole voyage he only saw one piece of natural driftwood and no other boats or aircraft.

Ideas from everyone

With awareness of plastic-free solutions still in its early stages, some of the issues we faced as individuals were downright hilarious – and expensive. In one instance I remember someone was horrified but too embarrassed to speak up when charged $17 for four sausages because the butcher didn't tare her glass Pyrex container and deduct the weight from the price. Our graphic designer Kate felt uncomfortable taking containers to be refilled, so we made name tags that said 'On a Plastic Free Diet'. The tags were recycled, but people kept pointing out that they were plastic (even though they were reusable), so Kate organised to have wooden ones engraved. 'I do remember how helpful it was to have the badges when approaching a butcher for the first time,' said Kate.

It was so exciting to see ideas emerging. A local high school student started making reusable produce bags from secondhand netting curtains, which helped many people tackle an early obstacle. This innovative approach was expanded by a participant organising a bag-making workshop at a local community hall. Another challenger organised a communal 'party kit' for 50 people with enough reusable bowls, plates, cups, utensils and cloth napkins for her friends and family to borrow. The solutions were inventive and sometimes unconventional. They had to be.

Importantly, we kept doing the challenge in our own lives. It was never about just trying to educate or change others. In those early days we personally knew many of the people participating and we got a lot of direct feedback. This helped us understand what people needed and the changes we could all make as individuals. What became known as Plastic Free July was developed by and with all the people participating. It spread by word of mouth, but we really had no idea how it spread so quickly and widely. What we did know is that when our group of like-minded colleagues and the 'Waste 101' crew set out to change ourselves and what went into our rubbish bins, we found that we increasingly connected to people's shared concerns. People *wanted* to make practical changes in their lives that responded to those concerns. We'd created an 'accidental campaign' that grew into something we could not have imagined.

In that second year, we garnered the support of 400 people not only from Australia, but from New Zealand, the US, Canada, the Netherlands and Egypt.

How do you take the challenge?

People often want to know the 'rules' of Plastic Free July. They ask about certain items or plastics that aren't single use, and some want a set of regulations. From the beginning, we tried to avoid that as much as possible and not be prescriptive about how to do the challenge. Plastic Free July is about learning to make small changes through choosing to refuse single-use plastics. It's not focused on changing everything at once and there is no such thing as 'failing' the challenge. We have people tell us stories of their 'failures' such as 'I've failed Plastic Free July because I went to a café and ordered a drink but it came with a plastic straw and I hadn't even thought about it'. Our response is always to encourage them and point out that if they had ordered that drink before taking the challenge they probably wouldn't have even noticed the straw. They have already made progress.

Making change can start with awareness, and a resolve to do things differently. We encourage people to start with the low-hanging fruit like bags and water bottles. Once you change those behaviours and form a habit, taking on a few additional items is more achievable so when you get to the end of July you may think, 'You know what? I can do without those things'. When you become more attuned to your plastic use and make adjustments to your purchasing habits, you are making progress. We try not to be too dogmatic because everyone's circumstances are different. In fact, our philosophy came to reflect this: *The change you try is your Plastic Free July.*

The process assists people to be far more aware of how much plastic there is in their lives and ultimately to discover new solutions. Doing the challenge involves each of us making a pact with ourselves. It holds us accountable. If you say, 'Oh, I forgot my reusable cup but I still want a takeaway coffee' in your day-to-day life, there are no consequences; it is easy to take the disposable option. When you are part of the challenge, it forces you to be mindful – going without is a powerful incentive to remember your reusable cup in future. I think that is what makes the challenge work – taking simple steps, one at a time. You choose something to forgo, then make it a habit, then move on to the next thing.

If we all do our bit, it adds up to a big impact. It's never been about being perfect. Some people can fit a year's worth of landfill waste into a jar – I'm not ashamed to admit that I'm not one of those people – but if we can all change our plastic use by 5 or 10 per cent, particularly those plastic items that litter our environment, then we start to tackle the issue as a conscious and committed society. At this stage, we were just a small group, but the changes we were noticing in our lives helped us to realise that you should never doubt the power of small actions. Of course we could not have envisaged that those small actions would grow into a community of millions.

> 'To be honest we've ebbed and flowed over the years, sometimes opting for convenience in busy times then resetting back to being mindful about our waste, but for the most part we've vastly reduced our consumption and waste creation since 2012. I buy most of my clothes at the charity store, we've got a bokashi bin, there's bulk food and bulk cleaning shops now just down the road from us ... and those cloth bags are still holding up a treat.'
>
> – Emma, Plastic Free July participant (since 2012), 2019

•

Plastic Free July shines a light on our unconscious habits, and leads us to question the norms in our societies that have enabled those behaviours to flourish. The solutions aren't just about remembering our reusables and they aren't just about reducing plastic either; eschewing the takeaway and dining in with our families and friends achieves far more than the obvious environmental benefits. Savouring a sit-down coffee in a ceramic cup is a lifestyle decision embraced in many European countries that Australians could certainly benefit from.

Plastic has become a symbol of our busy lives and our need to get a quick fix. In some ways it has enabled us to do everything at once, and that may make some aspects of life more efficient, but it certainly diminishes others in profound and lasting ways. Being present and intentional, and making thoughtful choices, have much in common with the plastic-free philosophy. Plastic may last forever, but we don't, so decisions that improve our quality of life are definitely worth pursuing.

3

The story of throwaway living

The numbers tell a story. We've only managed to recycle a mere 9 per cent of plastics ever made, and just 0.9 per cent have been recycled more than once.

People are often surprised by these low rates of recycling, but I think that there is a very small reason at the heart of this very big problem. Pick up random plastic-packaged items from a supermarket shelf and you will often find the tiny number I'm talking about. Look for a number between 1 and 7. It will be inside three chasing arrows forming a triangle, otherwise known as the universal recycling symbol.

Like me, you probably grew up thinking this recycling symbol indicated that the item would be recycled – it just needed to be put in the recycling bin. The numbers 1 to 7 do not mean that at all. They are actually 'resin identification codes' that tell us what type of plastic an item is made from. Number 1 is found on clear plastic water or soft-drink bottles and indicates the material is PET (or polyethylene terephthalate). Number 2, found on plastic milk bottles, is HDPE (high-density polyethylene). And so it goes until we reach number 7, which encompasses the growing category of 'other plastics'.

When the Society of the Plastics Industry introduced this code in

1988 and decided to enclose each number within a recycling symbol, it gave not only the wrong impression but also a false sense of hope. Though most plastics are technically recyclable, *are* they recycled? For myriad reasons, the answer is often 'no'. I think having the recycling symbol on plastic items has lulled consumers into a false sense of security, justifying our choices and purchases: 'It's okay to buy this – it's going to be recycled afterwards.'

Comparing the global plastics recycling rate of 9 per cent (calculated in 2017) with the rate of 70–90 per cent for steel or 58 per cent for paper offers an alarming perspective. That same year, China, a large importer of recyclable materials, announced its National Sword policy, which restricted the importation of some recycled materials. It also imposed strict contamination limits, meaning that other items such as plastic bags, nappies or plastic film that sometimes wrongly ended up in our recycling would no longer be tolerated. Alongside other countries, Australia had been exporting much of its recyclable waste overseas for reprocessing – including material from the recycling facility I first visited when I had my penny-drop moment. At that facility, recyclables are sorted into different material types, with plastics separated according to their resin identification codes.

Not all plastics are equal. Their value and their final destinations vary significantly. Plastics numbers 1 and 2 are typically the most valuable. Depending on current market prices and the quality of the material, recyclers usually make a profit from the processing of these materials, even after costs for sorting and transportation are taken into account. Plastics numbered 3 to 7 are often baled as mixed

> 'I think a lot of communities are really stepping up. They have to because China's not taking our plastic anymore.'
>
> – Jackie Nuñez, founder, The Last Plastic Straw

plastics, which are less useful materials and can be more difficult to find markets for. After local sorting and transport fees, the net result is often a cost to recycle if markets can be found. Previously the value of these mixed plastic bales was largely from the further sorting of the material; this happened overseas, where labour costs were lower, and where plastics 1 and 2 were extracted. Like other materials we produce in this country, such as wool, wheat and iron ore, plastics are also commodities, so their values vary and they are transported to where they will be reprocessed and used for manufacturing. A marginal amount of this happens in Australia. Most is destined for international markets.

When other countries importing recyclable materials followed China's lead and started refusing and even rejecting our exports, the result was an outcry. In Australia, this led to the closure of some of the materials recovery facilities that processed our recycling, so some councils were suddenly unable to offer recycling services to their residents. Even though these situations were sometimes only temporary, it did shake the community's faith in recycling. Images of shipping containers of contaminated waste being returned to our shores outraged conscientious recyclers and created scepticism: was all our recycling going to landfill? In some ways I think the National Sword decision was positive in that it shone a light on what was happening with our waste. Suddenly everyone wanted to talk about recycling; I couldn't even go to a dinner party without 'talking rubbish'. Plastics in particular were on the agenda.

Despite the challenges, taking responsibility for our own waste has the potential to create innovative solutions. Plans to establish onshore recycling facilities have since been announced. It feeds into a more receptive and responsible way of thinking and maybe an understanding that brings to mind an Indigenous perspective of our land: we are its caretakers for a limited period of time and the decisions we make have long-lasting impacts on future generations. In those rejected shipping containers were dirty nappies in paper bales and plastic bags wrapped up in bales of plastic bottles that *we* had put in there. We can do better. As consumers, we can all play a role by reducing our waste and being more diligent about sorting our recycling. And we are right to expect packaging manufacturers, business, the waste industry and government to play a role in fixing this recycling crisis.

'We need to move away from putting the cost and responsibility of recycling onto local governments and, ultimately, ratepayers, and put it back onto the producers of those items,' says Tim Youe, CEO of Southern Metropolitan Regional Council in Perth, which is responsible for managing the waste of almost 300 000 residents from four local council areas. (Its facility was where I'd had my penny-drop moment.) 'If producers are making packaging that we can't currently recycle, then that item should be on the shelves at greater cost and the consumer should be aware that it won't actually be recycled.'

Recycling costs money, Tim adds, and its costs are increasingly borne by the recycling industry – not manufacturers. 'The recycling industry bears the cost of putting in increasingly complex and expensive technology to process all these new types of packaging. Manufacturers of products need to make their products readily recyclable and, if not, they should not be given social licence to put their product into the market.'

Welcome to the throwaway society

The image shows a clean-cut, all-American family. The young daughter sports a cute frock and bobby socks, the father has a sharp 'do and the mother wears a swing skirt. All three are grinning euphorically, their arms raised in exaggerated joy. They fling TV dinner trays, plastic spoons, ice-cream tubs, straws and plates as

WORKING WITH OUR WASTE

Gunther Hoppe

CEO, Mindarie Regional Council, Perth; chair, Plastic Free Foundation

If you want to get up close and personal to the waste issue, a waste facility is a great place to start. Once we throw something in the bin, many of us don't give it a second thought, especially if we are fortunate enough to have our rubbish conveniently collected by our local council. Gunther Hoppe thinks about it, though. A lot. He 'stumbled into the waste game' several years ago, and now he is CEO of Mindarie Regional Council, a waste management authority in Perth that is responsible for processing the waste of seven local councils. He oversees Mindarie's Tamala Park waste facility, which operates 362 days a year and is one of the largest in Western Australia, taking in the refuse of roughly one-third of metropolitan Perth's 2 million people. Rubbish is Gunther's world and he's perfectly positioned to tell us where we're going wrong with it.

In Australia, landfill equates to almost 24 million tonnes of waste each year, a whopping 2400 kilograms per household. Waste facilities like the one at Mindarie tackle this rubbish – the stuff that no one else wants to deal with – after it is collected from residential waste bins and verges across the council area. The diversity of waste is only limited by your imagination. Alongside the contents of your average kitchen bin are appliances, weeds, clothes, disposable nappies and toxic e-waste. Much of it is strangled by plastic bags. The most unusual landfill contents? 'Whales and giraffes. If a giraffe at the local zoo dies, where else do you take it?' Gunther says.

At this site, the mountains of trash are dumped, spread, compacted and covered each day to reduce the odour and stop birds from scavenging. The plastic will be buried there forever. The organic matter breaks down but poses its own set of problems. Pipes extract the methane gas collected from decomposing organic matter; the gas is used to generate electricity and fed back into the grid to power local households. Unfortunately, there are still thousands of landfill sites across Australia that don't have this type of gas extraction infrastructure.

The wake-up call

So why are Australians creating millions of tonnes of waste each year? Before moving to Western Australia, Gunther worked in Malawi, a landlocked country in south-eastern Africa; in its developing-nation environment, reusable rubbish is seen as an opportunity, not a wasted luxury. 'If you were to knock down a house in Malawi, there would be five guys on their way to collect the bricks for another building job. It was a very different paradigm,' he reflects. 'When my family moved to Australia, we had a bulk verge collection and the stuff that people threw out spoke to a very opulent, consumerist society, which I hadn't seen outside the United States.'

'Be educated about the process'

Gunther is clear about how we can make a difference to the amount of waste we generate. 'We are over-consumers. You see it in how many TVs people have – three people and four to five TVs in one household. Buying less is an unpopular message in Australia, but the current approach is not sustainable. Self-imposed austerity or restraint around purchases is important.'

Education is making a difference. Over the last ten years, awareness has grown and this is leading to behaviour change. At the Tamala Park facility, most staff work in the 'recovery' space; it sounds like the perfect post-weekend-hangover haunt, but is instead a place where locals and businesses bring unwanted items that are able to be diverted out of landfill.

'We first and foremost encourage people to recycle and reuse,' he says. 'If you're not going to 'Gumtree' it, don't throw it out; bring it in and someone can give it a second life. The best thing we can do is not create waste in the first place, but if it does have to go in the bin, be educated about the process.'

The amount of waste going into landfill when Gunther started working at the Tamala Park facility was around 300 000 tonnes a year. Seven years later, that has dropped to around 180 000 tonnes a year.

though they are tossing confetti. This is a family on their way up in the world, rising above the grind of domesticity and into a life of convenience. Yes, the shiny, happy world of disposables is something to be embraced.

This image accompanied an article called 'Throwaway Living: Disposable items cut down household chores' in the August 1955 edition of *Life* magazine. It is often referred to as the first time the term 'throwaway society' was used. 'The objects flying through the air in this picture would take 40 hours to clean – except that no housewife need bother,' the author enthused. 'They are all meant to be thrown away after use.'

I can see why this was an attractive proposition at a time when there were fewer labour-saving appliances available in the home. Today it reads like satire, but is it really so far removed from the life of convenience many of us have grown up with? Isn't throwaway living the taken-for-granted existence of the past few generations? Are we only now fully starting to realise its impacts?

The idea of using items once and then throwing them away didn't come naturally. For the generations that lived through times of scarcity during the Great Depression and two world wars, thriftiness and careful use of resources were essential. I remember many years ago going to my mother-in-law's 80th birthday celebration, a large gathering of four generations for a picnic at the park. Drinks were served in disposable plastic cups – or so I thought. It turns out that they had been purchased back in 1969 for her eldest son's 21st birthday party. For each family event – and, being a large family, there were many – these cups were brought out, used, then carefully washed and stored for the next time.

Back in 1955, the idea of throwing items away after one use ran counter to normal living practices, so the producers of disposable products needed to encourage people to join the 'throwaway society'. The single-use way of thinking grew rapidly, in a short space of time.

Disposable plastic became so common that within a generation we'd stopped really noticing it and forgotten the simple alternatives. Fortunately, this is beginning to change.

> 'I remember my grandmother rinsing out her plastic bags and hanging them on the line to dry so she could reuse them. Now, if I ever get a plastic bag, I love rinsing it out and putting it on the line. It's my little connection to her.'
>
> – Sasha, Plastic Free July participant

The rise of plastics

Curious to understand how we'd come to be a throwaway society, I started looking into how plastics were made, and why they were invented in the first place. The word 'plastic' comes from the Greek verb *plassein*, which means to mould or to shape. Fossil fuels – oil, gas and coal – are the primary materials from which almost all plastics are made. Add plasticisers, stabilisers and other chemicals and they can take on an infinite number of forms limited only by our imagination. In the 21st century plastics are used in packaging, toys, clothing, computers, bicycle helmets, medical equipment, carpet, trains, planes and automobiles – the list is almost endless. It's hard to imagine a world without plastic.

The first synthetic plastics were designed a little over a century ago to replace materials in limited supply, such as ivory (from elephant tusks), amber (fossilised resin from trees) and tortoiseshell. The scarcity of those resources meant that items such as billiard balls, piano keys and hair combs were luxury commodities only available to a privileged few. One of the first human-made plastics was celluloid, invented in the 1860s and 1870s, which was derived from plant matter. An ideal material for hair combs, celluloid was inexpensive, unlike tortoiseshell; it didn't rust like metal, or become mouldy like wood; and it was sturdier than natural materials, but it could craftily be rendered to look like a natural material. Courtesy of celluloid, anyone could afford to buy a comb or even a whole vanity set that was both functional and beautiful with classical ivory-style markings. In 1907 the first plastic made from synthetic materials, Bakelite, was used in an even wider variety of items such as radio and telephone casings, kitchenware and household appliances.

More and more plastics were developed in Bakelite's wake, including polystyrene, nylon and polyvinyl chloride (PVC), but the thinking had shifted. As described by Susan Freinkel in *Plastic: A toxic love story*, scientists were moving on from materials that simply imitated nature to alternatives that creatively reworked nature. Production grew slowly but then nearly quadrupled during World War II as this new wonder material was put to use in the war effort, in everything from the pocket combs issued to the armed forces, to helmet liners and even the gun turrets where artillery was mounted. Post-war, this production needed to be adapted for non-military uses, and consumer markets were developed. Enter the throwaway society.

Plastic has become the symbol of the throwaway society not only because of how much we are producing and its excessive use in our lives, but because it is generally used only once before disposal. Unlike other materials we make, such as glass, metal and paper, plastics represent the first time in our history that we have used a resource en masse for a single occasion.

Deep in resource debt

The real picture of a throwaway society is of course bigger than plastic. It's the story of what happens when a growing population coincides with increasing manufacturing capability and the emergence of a consumer culture. The final chapter of the throwaway society ends with us gleefully throwing things into the bin after we've used them once. Yet this is the beginning of the story, not the end: a tale of landfill and litter.

It's worth stepping back for a moment to consider humanity's use of the Earth's resources as a whole. Facts and figures can be overwhelming and hard to relate to. Like many people, I'm a visual learner and find a picture helpful to understand an issue. The best method I've found to communicate our overuse of resources is called Earth Overshoot Day. Developed by the Global Footprint Network, Earth Overshoot Day estimates the date each year that humanity's consumption of ecological resources and services exceeds what the Earth can regenerate in that year. To calculate this, the Network creates a sort of global bank statement that tracks income (that is, supply – representing the biological productive land and sea areas) against expenditure (that is, the population's demand for those biological productive land and sea areas, including resources for food, materials and space, and outputs of waste and pollution).

We always want our bank statements to balance, and preferably we'd like our income to exceed our expenditure; this means we have money in the bank. What we want to avoid is spending more than we earn because then we are in debt. So, in an ideal world, we don't want Earth Overshoot Day to be on our calendar at all. We don't want to use more resources in any given year than the Earth can regenerate in that year. Unfortunately that hasn't happened since about the time Joanna and I were born. In 1970, Earth Overshoot Day fell on 29 December – not too bad, but still two days too early. As we kept using more and more resources, the date then got earlier each year. Almost 50 years later, in 2019, it arrived on 29 July, meaning that we were consuming almost twice what the planet can sustainably produce in one year. Ecological bankruptcy is upon us, and it is not an occasion we want to celebrate among the usual good-news stories at the end of Plastic Free July.

We need to keep this picture in mind as we explore the plastics problem and start to turn towards solutions. Every item that is manufactured uses resources and has a cost, so switching from single-use plastics to single-use items manufactured from other materials might address a litter issue – but it doesn't necessarily change the bigger problem that we are just consuming too much. That also applies to buying new reusables in this season's style and colours, no matter how attractive they are. We always encourage people doing Plastic Free July to use what they have or buy secondhand where possible. Resources are used at every stage along the chain: extracting raw materials, then manufacturing, producing, transporting, selling, using and disposing of goods. *All* products use resources, whether they are designed to be used once – such as a plastic bag or a compostable bag made from corn – or designed for multiple uses, such as a cotton tote bag. The big picture is that we need to get back in balance and move the Earth Overshoot date later. There is no other way to do this than by reducing what we are 'spending', that is, what we are consuming. Our Plastic Free July ethos around this has always been to buy what you need and buy to last. In the challenge, we start with plastics; this leads to being mindful and questioning consumption in other areas.

Indigenous perspectives on waste

It's useful to step back and consider the current scale of our plastics problem from a historical perspective. After all, it wasn't invented that long ago and our consumer culture is a relatively recent development. In Australia white colonisation introduced a mindset of land and resource 'ownership' that was in stark contrast to the way that Indigenous Australians had lived on the land for tens of thousands of years.

> 'This is our time in history to start [Earth Overshoot Day] moving backwards at a faster and faster rate. It is possible to reduce our consumption, reuse and recycle our waste and eventually begin regenerating all the damaged ecosystems caused by us. This is the agenda for our moment in time.'
>
> – Professor Peter Newman AO, Professor of Sustainability, Curtin University; lead author, Intergovernmental Panel on Climate Change (IPCC)

These traditional owners have been custodians of Australia for more than 2400 generations and have acted upon a sacred duty to care for the land. The raw materials used for housing, food, tools and clothing came from the land and were returned to it in line with that sacred duty. Worimi woman Nadine Russell, from the New South Wales Hunter region, describes the relationship: 'We don't own the land, the land owns us. We are not merely custodians, we are here to protect the land and ensure it's not damaged, ensure there's a legacy for the next generation.'

Colonisation occurred 230 years ago, and the first plastics were invented around 150 years ago. In this historically brief timeframe (a mere five generations), as has happened around the world, Australia's mainstream culture has come to accept a material that will last forever as a disposable commodity.

Ingrid Cumming, a Whadjuk Noongar woman from Fremantle, learned about boodjar (the land) and her place within it from her community. 'My elders taught me, when you go into a place you have to leave it as you found it. When I go onto Country and work with people, this cultural component is ESSENTIAL. It is an honour to carry on that work of my ancestors as a custodian of Whadjuk Noongar Country.

'As I've grown up and connected more with cultural knowledge, I've learned how it was a sustainable culture and how most resources from Country had multiple uses. We are taught to always use as much as possible of plants or animals, not just one part and then throw it away. A balga or grass tree, for example, had a hundred different uses.'

Ingrid now works as the Aboriginal advisor for Western Australia's Return Recycle Renew, which will coordinate the container deposit scheme in Western Australia. 'It blows my mind the amount of plastics I have seen in the water on my travels, and just how bad the plastics situation is in places,' Ingrid says. 'When I do a

Welcome to Country, it's a chance for me to reconnect and connect others to Country. If we aren't connected to Country, we can get sick. We need to look after our Country, to keep it healthy, to keep ourselves healthy and leave behind only our footprints.'

In New Zealand, Jacqui Forbes is the general manager of Para Kore (Zero Waste), an organisation that delivers waste education programs to the sacred meeting grounds (*marae*) in Māori communities. Para Kore was one of the first organisations I'd heard of doing Plastic Free July in New Zealand, so we have shared several conversations over the years. Jacqui always speaks about the connection in Māori culture between people and the land and the way it informs an alternative response to the concept of waste.

'It's about wanting to lead change, but wanting to do that from the Māori world view. This comes from Māori culture, values, beliefs and assumptions and also from our stories that have been passed down,' Jacqui says.

In Māori cultures, the relationships between land and humans are intimate. 'The Earth is our mother and the sky is our father. We are related to mountains, to rocks, to insects, to birds, to the rivers and bush, to all parts of the natural world. They are our ancestors, our relations. We are the *teina*, the younger sibling, and therefore we are just part of nature. We identify with landforms and the place, but also with the spiritual realms,' Jacqui explains.

Custodianship of the land is passed down through generations, and the relationship is reciprocal: you look after the land and the land looks after you. 'Reciprocity is a highly regarded value within *te ao Māori* [the Māori world],' Jacqui says. 'When we are sending everything to landfill, we are not looking after Mother Earth. We're burying our rubbish and she can't digest it. We're kind of poisoning her.'

Para Kore focuses on changing behaviour and systems through mentoring and supporting Māori communities, and providing education and practical skills including bin audits (similar to our Earth

WASTE IN THE WHOLE COMMUNITY

Vandana K

New Delhi, India

Journalist, producer, sustainability blogger and Plastic Free July participant Vandana K lives in New Delhi, and describes her interest in waste – particularly plastic waste – as an 'incremental learning journey' that started as personal change making and spread to advocacy and community support. The story of waste in India, as in many other places, cannot be separated from its historical and social context.

India's waste system

Historically, in India, waste was reallocated; items were repaired and people lived frugally. This circular system meant that waste was dealt with efficiently.

'Consumption where I am from was limited and people were very focused on their basic necessities,' Vandana says. 'Houses would have an area out the back with a bin-like structure where people could dump their waste, mostly vegetable peels, and that would be made available to the cows. Everything was sold in big jute sacks and people would bring their cloth bags and fill them with groceries.'

With the growth of cities and migration to those areas, India set up more formal infrastructure for waste management, and cities such as Delhi and Mumbai developed a waste management system over time. Internal migration and unchecked growth of settlements has expanded these cities and now the system is under tremendous pressure.

'Every city has a municipal corporation responsible for processing waste and collecting. Each neighbourhood has an area demarcated for waste collection, which is a concrete structure,' Vandana explains. These basic structures have two large waste containers marked green for biodegradable material and brown for mixed waste. In urban areas like New Delhi, household waste is collected daily and loaded into pushcarts or rickshaws for delivery to waste collection areas.

'Most often waste workers are Dalits (people considered to be from a low caste who have been oppressed for centuries under the caste system) and minorities. Waste work is done by men, women and also children.'

The majority of rural areas and small towns still lack a proper system of waste management. In poorer neighbourhoods with unauthorised colonies, there are usually no such waste-disposal facilities. Locals need to find their own way to dispose of waste. Informal waste disposal practices such as burning or dumping into the drains and waterways are sometimes the only options. 'I think maybe people feel that it will float away to nothingness, but it goes to the rivers and then the sea; this still happens,' Vandana says. She notes that the Yamuna River – the second-largest tributary of the Ganges – is suffering. 'It is in very poor condition. Apart from all the effluent from factories and sewage from homes it also gets a lot of waste related to rituals and special ceremonies.'

Traditionally, ceremonial items such as marigold flowers were biodegradable. The sacred material was placed in the river as a way of returning it to nature. Now these items are packaged in plastic; when they are dumped into the river at the end of riverside rituals, the toll on India's waterways is devastating.

'I have to talk about the waste workers'

Vandana once spent a day following a local waste worker from her neighbourhood to witness the system firsthand. Once the mixed garbage is collected, it is sorted and recyclable materials are separated. Waste collectors gather piles of plastic and they are cycled to an informal waste processing unit where they live. These areas may have no running water. The waste workers gather the plastic outside their homes and waste buyers on-sell it to contractors where further material segregation takes place. It is again sold, compacted into bales and sent to recycling factories on the outskirts of cities, where it is converted into plastic pellets and then recycled into cheap materials such as buckets and stools.

'All the scavenged plastic can be resold. PET bottles can earn waste collectors 15 to 30 rupees (about 20–60 Australian cents) per kilo which is very important as a source of income. Food waste is sometimes sold to an animal shelter. Cardboard and glass are resold too,' Vandana says. Valueless items including bottle caps, plastic wire and disposables like cups or plastic cutlery don't make it to the recycling unit and these are destined for landfill.

Vandana believes simply removing plastic from the economy is not the answer unless there is a workable alternative in place. 'A huge number of waste workers are dependent on plastic to survive. These people are earning 200 to 300 rupees a day' – A$4–6, approximately – 'and they would lose that,' she points out. The plastics issue cannot exist in isolation from the communities involved, the economic systems and social and equity issues.

> 'Most people don't know who their waste worker is and they are usually only paid a minimal wage. I have to talk about the waste workers otherwise it is an incomplete account,' Vandana says. 'Especially in the context of India, the story has to include who collects your waste and what happens to them if a new system is put in place.'

Carer audits). As with Plastic Free July, their ethos is to empower people, rather than simply tell them what they *should* do, or do it for them. Empowerment is much more likely to succeed in the long term.

Masses of plastic

In 2017, the first ever global study of how the world's plastic production and use, and where it ultimately ended up, revealed some devastating findings. The study's authors found plastic production had outgrown most other human-made materials.

You only have to glance down any aisle of a supermarket to see those findings in action; we know plastic production is growing rapidly. Despite this, the actual figures are staggering. Since mass plastic production began just 60 years ago, 8.3 billion metric tonnes of plastic has been produced, much of it used in disposable products. That is more than one metric tonne for every person in our global population. As of 2015 around 9 per cent had been recycled, 12 per cent incinerated, and 79 per cent accumulated in landfills or the natural environment. This exponential increase in production would surely 'break' any system that was not prepared to manage it. Leakages from the waste management systems were inevitable.

The news of this low recycling rate received a lot of attention and was a rallying statistic for Plastic Free July. How can we feel good about tossing plastic into the recycling bin when we are landfilling and even incinerating more plastic waste than we are recycling? The amount recycled more than once was, as mentioned earlier, just 0.9 per cent of all plastics made. Instead of being continually recycled, most plastic is 'downcycled' to lesser quality products, which are in turn less likely to be recycled. After being sorted into different polymer types, plastics are shredded, washed and melted into pellets to be made into new products. In the case of plastic bottles the recycled plastic can be spun into yarn to become synthetic clothing, and food packaging can be processed to make new bollards or decking, but what happens to these items at the end of their lives? What about the next use, and the next?

One of the key problems is that manufacturers, producers and designers of goods have largely been looking only at their own little parts of the production and consumption chain, without considering how their products will be used or disposed of further along the chain. Perhaps visiting waste and recycling facilities should be part of training to give industrial creators and makers their own penny-drop moment. The problems are particularly evident with plastics. Although the resin codes – those numbers inside the three-arrow symbols – identify the basic material type, there are thousands of other chemicals that can be added. And different types of plastic can also be mixed together. Juice boxes, for example, can be made of multiple layers of paper and aluminium foil, with plastic polyethylene forming both the innermost layer (so that liquid is fully contained) and a protective coating on the exterior (keeping the package dry and providing a printing surface). This is a recycling challenge even without the plastic straw affixed to the side of the box with plastic film – an additional two material types, and two common litter items. It is good to see some packaging companies are starting to address these challenges.

> 'Where packaging is required, it is imperative that it is designed using circular principles – choosing materials with a minimal footprint, creating efficiencies in their use, and maximising the potential for the material to be recovered back into the economy via recycling.'
>
> – Detpak, sustainable packaging manufacturer

A replacement mentality

When we think of 'single-use' items, we typically classify them as things like plastic plates, cups, cutlery and packaging. Yet there is now a growing grey area of items that were originally made to be durable and long-lasting but are now often used only a couple of times. These items are usually cheap to replace or seen as inconvenient to store away. The 'waste' being left behind at music festivals is a perfect example – tents can be purchased for as little as $20, camp chairs can be purchased for just $5 and some leisure inflatables are easier to replace than reinflate. Consumer goods are now being sold so cheaply that replacing them instead of reusing them becomes the default position.

Planned obsolescence is a way to describe this 'designed for the dump' approach where items are created with an artificially limited life span. Think of those products whose replacement parts are simply not available, or whose replacement parts cost more than buying a brand new product, and then consider the obvious benefits to manufacturers and retailers of ongoing sales. Even being aware of

> 'As a society we have started to treat products once considered durable items as single-use conveniences.'
>
> – Gunther Hoppe, CEO, Mindarie Regional Council, Perth

this tactic doesn't mean we can avoid it: though I have tried to buy quality toasters, none of them ever seems to last beyond a few years. The toaster my in-laws were given as a wedding present lasted decades. *Perceived obsolescence*, on the other hand, is when a customer is convinced of the 'need' for an updated product, even though the existing one is fully functional. Constantly updated mobile phone models with new features are an example of this.

Among Plastic Free July participants, our conversations have extended beyond simply reducing single-use plastics to considering what we *need* versus what we *want*. Selecting durable, quality items is an important part of pushing back against a disposable mindset.

The heart of the plastics problem

When I refer to the 'problem' of plastics, I'm referring to plastic *waste*. Plastic waste is what doesn't get recycled; it's the plastics that end up in landfill or are incinerated or leach out of waste management systems and litter the environment, waterways and ultimately the oceans. In my mind it looks like this:

> Plastic production – Plastic recycling = Plastic waste (including pollution)

The fundamental problem is the plastic waste that results from the ways we are using (and not reusing) plastic. Plastic is lightweight, cheap, durable and adaptable, and therefore it is all too easy to simply use and throw away. But those same qualities make it a valuable material in many areas of everyday life – in the transportation, communications, medical and clothing industries, to name a few. In the early days of Plastic Free July we would always say to people 'Keep taking your medications! We don't want any medical emergencies or unwanted pregnancies from people forgoing plastic during the challenge'. The focus of Plastic Free July has always been on the unnecessary wastage we've cultivated through our throwaway society culture of convenience, and we acknowledge the value it can have – such as in the medical industry, or delivering food aid or clean water supplies.

In our messaging we also tried to communicate the differences between our linear use of plastics and the way that organic materials cycle through natural ecosystems. During those first years of the plastic-free challenge, a lot of the conversation focused on how long a plastic bag or water bottle takes to 'break down'. But unlike a tree shedding leaves, which then decompose on the forest floor

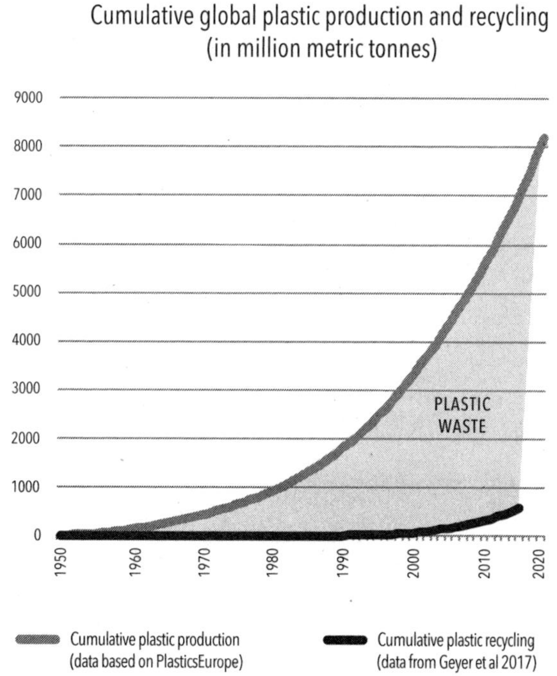

and return nutrients back into the soil for new growth, plastics don't break down – they just break up into smaller and smaller pieces and remain in the environment.

•

The consequences of ever-increasing plastic production are overwhelming, and the problem is set to grow. Over the last decade fracking shale gas has made producing the raw materials for plastics significantly cheaper, and at the same time the demand for fossil fuels has waned with the switch to renewable energy and battery power. The result is exponential growth – plastic production is expected to double again in 20 years and almost quadruple by 2050 (*New Plastics Economy*). If this plastic continues to be manufactured into single use without adequate waste management systems, the repercussions of our throwaway society for our planet and ourselves are far beyond anything we can imagine.

4

Tackling the Top 4

When Sue Herbert was growing up in York, England, the essential food items that her family needed were delivered to her door. The fruit man came around with his cart, the milkman ladled milk into jugs and, when Sue was first married, the fishmonger would visit their home in his van.

'He would come into our village one day a week. When you went to get your fresh fish, you took your plate out,' she remembers.

In later years, Sue would often shop on her way home from work at small stores. The lack of variety wasn't an issue because it was all that people knew. 'There was one type of sugar. If you wanted sugar, you just got white sugar.

'Going to the grocery shop was terribly relaxing. I sat on a stool on my side of the counter with my shopping list, and the grocer had pre-cut squares of thick brown paper to wrap dry goods. Honestly, he could fold that paper into a bag in the twinkling of an eye.

'I carried the shopping in a wicker basket and later on the basket of the pram. You bought your bread with a piece of paper around it, and the butcher used to wrap meat in paper. Other than fish and chips, which you got in newspaper, there was no takeaway food and no containers. If you went to a café you always had proper cutlery and crockery. If you were lucky enough to get a lemonade, you often got a paper straw.'

In the 1970s, when Sue moved to Australia, she started going to the supermarket. Initially her groceries were packed in a couple of thick paper bags. 'Most people had their own bags and baskets,' she says. 'I don't really remember much plastic packaging, but it started to escalate after the 1970s.

'My children didn't ever have their own water bottles, despite going to school in tropical north Queensland. There were water bubblers at school and they just used those. Sandwiches were wrapped in greaseproof paper and packed in lunch boxes.'

One lifestyle change Sue has noticed since then is the way people seem to be perpetually eating. 'People nowadays have always got food or drink in their hands,' she observes. Plastic packaging has created an 'eating and drinking on the go' mentality, blurring the boundaries of mealtimes and enabling a seemingly insatiable need to consume.

What are the Top 4?

Sue Herbert is my aunt. Though she is now in her late seventies, her memories of how people used to buy food and dine out in the pre-plastic era are crystal clear. Sue's insights helped me to realise that shopping without the convenience of plastic was just the way things were for *all* people in the not-too-distant past. It was really about keeping things simple. People weren't overwhelmed with choice.

In early 2013, when we were about to run Plastic Free July for the third time, we realised we needed to focus on those values of simplicity and ease of choice to encourage the general public to participate. My colleague and fellow Earth Carers coordinator Amy Warne came up with an idea to offer participants in Plastic Free July the option of just taking on what she called the 'Top 4' – plastic bags, plastic water bottles, plastic straws, and disposable cups and lids.

When we used the term 'plastic free' with fellow Earth Carers, they knew we were focusing on single-use plastic, but doing a challenge called 'Plastic Free July' may have seemed a bit extreme or unachievable to the general public. The Top 4 was like 'Plastic Free Lite' – a park run instead of a marathon – and it recognised that for newcomers to waste reduction, it was still a conceptual jump. Our Top 4 challenge helped people to start with the main plastics that were used on a regular basis and that were relatively easy to refuse or find alternatives for.

'People now understand the whole concept of single-use, but they didn't back then,' Amy remembers. '*I* didn't. It wasn't a common mindset.

'Looking back, in those days all the ideas we had were radical. When you took your own Tupperware containers to get Friday-night takeaway in the early years, they were really hard conversations to have. People looked at you like you were speaking another language. There was just no comprehension.'

A simple idea

The brilliance of the Top 4 was its simplicity. It focused on four common items used all over the world that could be tackled without too much effort or even any cost. Plastic Free July is only three words but the philosophy takes time to explain. With the Top 4, no matter where people lived or what they did, they could easily visualise the problem and the solution. Plastic bags, bottles, straws and cups distilled what was at the heart of the issue, and became clear symbols of the problem. They were highly visible, and the alternatives helped to convey the ideas of participation, change and a new norm.

The Top 4 was also a practical way of getting the message out. In those early years of Plastic Free July, we had no budget, and our means of engaging people had always been quite folksy. All our idea-sharing was dreamed up in-house using family photos and basic

> 'When our family participated in Plastic Free July, we decided to start with simple steps and see where that would take us. We stopped using plastic bags altogether and kept a collection of reusable bags on hand. This made us realise how conscious choices in our plastic use could have a bigger impact, so we stopped using other plastics such as cling film (replaced with brown paper bags and beeswax wraps), disposable coffee cups, and we reduced buying items in plastic packaging by bulk buying from the wholefood shop or making our own. We also bought food in glass jars so we could re-use them for pantry storage.'
>
> – Chontelle, Plastic Free July participant

sketches. We bodged things together with whatever we had on hand. But the Top 4 offered a visual simplicity that was easy to communicate. Other single-use plastics, such as food and beverage packaging, differ greatly between countries and cultures, as do the alternatives available. In many places, avoiding single-use plastics by buying in bulk is still not an option. In contrast, the Top 4 were ubiquitous, universal and largely avoidable wherever you were.

What really resonated was the uptake of the idea once we broke it down to that level, and how relatively uncomplicated it was for people to be involved. Because people may have already been focusing on one of the Top 4, it also made them feel that they were already succeeding and making a contribution, and that they could add in other items to extend their participation. While choosing to refuse takeaway containers involves preparation, planning and weathering the 'Are you a weirdo?' looks, there's nothing socially awkward or expensive about avoiding the Top 4. Our focus was and always will be on doing what you can, rather than focusing on the things you *can't* do. The power of the Top 4 was that if everyone just did that, it would make a significant dent in our reliance on single-use plastic and provide a gateway for participants to take the challenge further.

Small ask, big impact

Keeping the 'ask' small, keeping it simple, and getting lots of people to do what they can was far more productive for us than being overly prescriptive or rigid and only appealing to a few. Having this relatively easy entry point meant the challenge grew even more quickly. The Top 4 are not only items that we tend to use frequently and in large numbers in public places, they are unfortunately the ones that end up as litter. These were the items that we kept retrieving in our beach clean-ups. It was also a useful tool for people trying to spread the plastic-free message further. They could choose one of the four items and just focus on reducing that in their own community, at events or working with businesses. Over the years other environmental organisations and bloggers captured this message, and social media memes promoting the Top 4 or the renamed 'Big Four' started to appear, spreading via the grapevine and becoming somewhat of a phenomenon.

Number 1: The plastic bag

For an item that was only invented in the mid-1960s and wasn't widely produced until the 1970s, it's remarkable how popular the now-pervasive plastic shopping bag has become. Plastic bags are lightweight and durable, and are often made from polyethylene that is itself a waste product from crude oil refining and natural gas; this makes them incredibly cheap and therefore plentiful. Plastic bags are

> 'When looking to go zero waste, dipping your toe into waste reduction, or being more eco-friendly, my first suggestion is always the Big Four! The Big Four are four simple, easy swaps popularised by Plastic Free July.'
>
> – Kathryn Kellogg, author and zero-waste blogger

one of the most ubiquitous consumer products on the planet. That astounds me. Is that really a legacy we want to leave behind? Is it what we want to be remembered for by future generations?

Bags were an obvious choice for the Top 4 and a relatively easy place for people to start. Most of us already have lots of alternatives in our homes, though reusable bags are only reusable if people remember to take them. One day, on a whim, I decided to do a stocktake of reusable shopping bags in my home. On my kitchen table I spread out my favourite lightweight bags (made from recycled plastic bottles), half a dozen larger branded 'green bags', several insulated supermarket bags, calico bags from conferences and events, handmade bilums from Papua New Guinea, jute bags, homemade bags from my niece and nephew and community workshops, and my farmers' market basket that I used each Sunday. Fortunately we have a big table; there were 27 in total. The 'bag audit' resulted in me telling my family it was time we implemented a ban on accepting any new reusable bags. We had enough to last a lifetime.

The easiest and best solution is to use what you have and not be tempted to buy more reusable bags at the checkout, no matter how eco-friendly they seem. If you take the challenge and forget your reusable bags, the payback is coming out of a store awkwardly cradling groceries. That's usually enough of a deterrent.

> 'Why would you make something that you're going to use for a few minutes out of a material that's basically going to last forever, and you're just going to throw it away? What's up with that?'
>
> – Jeb Berrier, in *Bag It* (2010)

Which bag is best?

We are often asked 'What is the best type of bag?' The simple answer is 'the one you already have', but not all bags are created equal. When you start to compare material types and analyse a bag's life cycle, it quickly gets complicated.

Take the 'green bags' you can buy at the supermarket checkout, for example. They are usually made from non-woven polypropylene, a plastic that is technically recyclable but usually isn't. Difficult to wash, these bags are often disposed of after a few uses. Because they are cheap to produce, they are sold at supermarkets for a very small fee, or branded and given away by stores and other groups. Due to the materials and energy required to make them (more than a standard single-use plastic bag), they need to be used many times to offset this. Estimates of the number of times a reusable bag needs to be used to offset production costs vary widely, depending on the data used.

Even the paper grocery bag is not without impact. At face value, it is a more ethical and logical alternative to the plastic shopping bag. Made from natural materials, a paper bag is obviously going to break down more quickly if it is littered in the environment. A well-made paper bag can be reused, and if it is disposed of correctly it can be recycled. Yet paper bags are usually made from virgin paper from harvested trees; even those brown, natural-looking 'kraft paper' bags are mostly made from virgin paper. Even if sustainably sourced, there is still energy and resources used in making the bag.

Then there are bags made from cotton and calico. These have a much bigger carbon footprint than plastic bags, and it is estimated that each one needs to be used at least 130 times to offset this.

I'm not suggesting that we don't use paper bags or that plastic bags are in any way superior to paper or calico bags; it's important, though, to be aware that every item we produce uses resources and has impacts during its manufacture and disposal. The research and

PUT YOUR BAGS TO WORK

Keep reusable bags in a handy place and ready to use - we keep ours anywhere that will prevent our family from being caught out without one. Here are some more tips, including some from Plastic Free July participants:

- Keep bags with your keys and have a stash in your car boot.
- Hang some near the front door.
- Clip a bag in every purse/handbag, laptop cover and backpack.
- Have one in your work or study bag, or handbag.
- Shove a bag in your carry-on luggage when travelling.
- If you ever do need to purchase a bag, choose a durable and/or sustainably made one.
- Buy bags secondhand from thrift/charity/op shops.

reports on the life cycle of different kinds of bags are difficult to navigate but the important thing to understand is simply that any reusable bags need to be used many times to offset their production costs. This is why (repeat after me) using then reusing and reusing and reusing what we already have is *always* the best option.

At the end of the day, it's really quite simple. Remember the bag.

Number 2: The disposable water bottle

Imagine the pure genius of a marketing campaign that could convince people to buy something that they could already get for free. Unlike plastic bags that burst (sometimes literally) into our lives in the 1970s as a convenient replacement for paper bags, the 'luxury'

BANNING THE BAG

Nick Morrison

Co-founder, 'Bags Not', Auckland, New Zealand

Nick Morrison has been driving change in New Zealand in a major way. 'Bags Not' is a nationwide campaign to target shoppers' bag habits. It started when Nick began to take stock of his own plastic bag usage in 2012.

The wake-up call

'Plastic bags were my gateway, as they are for many people, into plastic pollution,' Nick remembers. 'At the time I was living in London and I was at a supermarket buying my groceries and reading a newspaper article that had a pretty impactful photo about plastic bags going into landfill. I was holding a plastic bag with my groceries and I just had a realisation that this was a massive problem and, holy shit, I was part of it.'

Plastic Free July came into Nick's life in what he describes as 'a heightened period of alertness'. At the time he was the only one of his friends taking on the challenge. 'Thinking about it now, I remember feeling quite on my own with it. It was great I did Plastic Free July because one of the beautiful things about social media is that you can connect with people outside your immediate friend group.'

Bananas in the hood

Nick recalls the first challenge as being a lot harder than he thought it would be. As a fitness trainer, he was used to the convenience of eating when he could between clients, but he was determined to see out the challenge.

'I was a bit naive at first, I guess. I remember it being so much harder than I had anticipated. Going into the supermarket, there were about five items in the veggie section I could buy. I remember almost going hungry for a couple of days.

'I was a "grab food on the go" kind of person – all the sandwiches and lunch options were wrapped in plastic. I think my food bill went up a bit because I would go to a café instead of buying takeaway. Then I started making my own lunches, with leftovers.'

Being one of the early adopters of the challenge, Nick remembers the strange looks he'd get in the early days. 'In London you have to have a backpack, so I would just shove stuff in there or cradle my groceries. Often I was wearing a hoodie, so I could put my bananas in there. I did get some looks.

'Based on my flatmates' lack of buy-in, they probably thought I was a bit weird, but it definitely sparked discussions. It was a good conversation starter.'

'Bags Not'

These personal changes were instrumental in Nick coming to terms with the broader plastic pollution problem. He travelled through South and Central America before returning to New Zealand to confront the single-use plastic bag issue head on.

'I vividly remember my experience on one of the small islands that make up the archipelago known as the San Blas Islands, off the north coast of Panama, where we took a break from our boat journey. The island was postcard perfect with crystal-clear water and golden sand on one side, but when I took a short walk to the other side of the island, I was confronted with plastic strewn as far as you could see. It was a profound experience. I wanted to put energy into solving the problem rather than being part of it.'

After changing his own purchasing behaviours, Nick was offered a job at sustainable packaging company Innocent Packaging. He started writing letters to his environment minister about ditching single-use plastic bags and one of these letters made it into the hands of advertising agency BCG2. The end result was 'Bags Not', a major New Zealand campaign that focused on the 'ridiculousness' of single-use plastic bags.

'It's not an effort anymore'

Nick is now plastic free from January to December.

'It gets down to a personal level and what your values are,' Nick says. 'Do you want to leave a place better than the way you found it? It's about taking a bit of personal responsibility.

'Plastic Free July had a big impact on me in terms of solidifying that behaviour change and it put me in good stead to go into "Bags Not" knowing what was possible, and knowing what it was like learning the behaviours yourself. I make a real effort but it's not an effort anymore – it is part of who I am. It is my normal.'

There is always room to improve, but taking on just one single-use plastic item can lead to lifelong changes. 'I want to come clean: I'm by no means perfect,' Nick says. 'There are still times I buy something in plastic but it's down to such a minimal amount now. I think that's the important message. We don't have to be completely plastic free; we don't have to be perfect. It is really challenging and there are still a lot of [non-plastic] products that are more expensive or harder to get – especially for people living outside of bigger cities. But just stop using water bottles, for one. Just stop using plastic bags. Don't worry if you forget one day. Don't quit. Keep getting better.'

Major New Zealand supermarket chains banned single-use plastic shopping bags in 2018 and 2019. The New Zealand Government implemented a national ban in 2019, a transition that Nick describes as 'pretty smooth'.

of bottled water has crept into our psyche more gradually, filling a need that, for most of us, didn't actually exist.

The contemporary marketing success story of bottled water has a precedent. Water has been bottled since the 17th century when visiting spas and 'water therapy' were in vogue, and drinking water from mineral springs was regarded as a healthy option. Commercial sales of bottled water followed, carbonated water was invented and sales grew – accompanied by concerns at that time about the safety of drinking water from unreliable municipal supplies. (This is still a very real threat in areas where cholera and typhoid outbreaks occur.)

Despite widespread improvements in public water supplies, though, the popularity of bottled water increased over the centuries, propelled by sophisticated marketing and advances in bottle manufacturing. Glass became the vessel of choice; in fact, it was the only option, and glass bottles were a valuable resource, routinely collected by the public and businesses and returned to beverage companies, who paid out small cash rewards through voluntary systems. It was a cost-effective and workable way to refill and reuse the bottles and this refill system still operates in many European countries.

In 1973, DuPont engineer Nathaniel Wyeth patented polyethylene terephthalate (PET) bottles, the clear plastic bottles used today for bottled water and carbonated soft drinks. (Today these are identified by the resin identification number 1.) Like plastic bags, PET bottles were lightweight and cheap to produce. These weren't the first plastic bottles ever made but they were the first to withstand the pressure of carbonated liquids, to resist breakage and to have an attractively clear surface. Today the PET bottle has replaced glass as the preferred material for single-serve bottled water.

Bottled water companies had a task in front of them. They had to convince us to buy something available on tap, and they did it through masterful packaging and promotion. They made us believe bottled water was healthier, had a superior taste and offered a connection to alluring destinations – such as 'natural artesian' water from Fiji, or 'pure' water from the Alps. Suggestive motifs of mountains, branding that included references to nature, and terminology like 'pristine' and 'as nature intended' enhanced the appeal. They succeeded, but at what price? Apart from the cost of extracting, packaging and transporting water and equity issues, what about the environmental implications? Aside from the carbon footprint involved, producing single-use water bottles for countries with ready

> 'Water should be abundant if it is treated with care. That bottled water was successfully marketed to areas of the planet that do have access to good drinking water is horrible. It's tantamount to bottling air. Water is life, and they've managed to put it into a bottle and sell it back to us and use it as such a status symbol that people are now completely blind to how much harm it causes the environment.'
>
> – Berish Bilander, co-CEO and campaigner, Green Music Australia

access to clean drinking water was a clear win for consumerism over rationality.

Long before the introduction of PET bottles, people had been carrying water in reusable bottles and containers made from clay, glass, steel and eventually plastic, but the PET bottle was a victory for convenience. Whether playing a sport, swimming at the beach or sitting in a meeting, single-serve bottled water was often a quick and, compared to other bottled drinks on the market, cheap option. For some it was a choice due to concerns about taste, or chlorine and fluoride treatments of public water. Freshness, purity, health and happiness were just a swig away, as long as we, and the planet, were willing to pay the price. To date we have been. In Australia, the bottled water industry generates over $700 million a year.

Doing what we can

Like the plastic bag, bottled water was an obvious item for Plastic Free July to target. After all, many people already had reusable water bottles and, if not, the alternatives were both well known and readily available. Most Australians have access to safe drinking water, so it was an item that could be avoided without too much effort.

That is not the case in some other parts of the world. There are places where safe drinking water supplies are limited and sometimes non-existent, and in those cases bottled water might be the only option. When Vandana K from New Delhi, India, joined in on Plastic Free July, she shared a photo of the plastic waste she had created during the first two weeks of the challenge. Vandana had reduced her plastic waste down to the plastic wrapping and seals of four reusable 20-litre bottles and one five-litre single-use plastic bottle of water.

'I live in an area that faces water shortages and contamination,' Vandana said at the time. 'I switched to a stainless steel ceramic filter earlier this year but if water mixed with sewage is flowing through your tap, even a filter can't do much. Just like many people in my neighbourhood and across urban India, I had to rely on privatised drinking water which comes in reusable and refillable 20-litre bottles.

'Water is the most basic human need and I am grateful I still have access to it. My intention for Plastic Free July is to do my best in my current context.'

Living in an apartment up four flights of stairs, Vandana found that deliveries are sometimes challenging. She had to buy the five-litre bottle on the day the delivery person didn't show up. She had no choice but to use it for drinking, cooking and washing dishes.

By participating in Plastic Free July, Vandana did what she could, where she was, and with what she had. That has always been our approach and it really highlights the opportunities many of us have to make relatively simple changes. Turning on a tap to access fresh drinking water wasn't an option for Vandana, but it *is* an option in countries like Australia. Our ability to avoid bottled water is a choice we shouldn't take for granted.

When we started the Top 4 initiative, reusable water bottles were already a known alternative, readily available and in a range of sizes, shapes and materials – glass, stainless steel, plastic sports-style

BOTTLE TIPS

- Take your own water bottle wherever you go, and fill it with tap or filtered water.
- Keep it in a handy location so you don't forget it.
- Use whatever bottle you have for as long as you can. When you need to upgrade, find a reusable bottle that suits your lifestyle.
- Bottles don't need to be fancy; you can even repurpose a glass jar or bottle.

MAKING MUSIC GREEN

Berish Bilander

Co-CEO and campaigner, Green Music Australia, Melbourne

When Berish Bilander lived in Jakarta, he was 'really shocked' at the extent to which the damaging elements of western culture had permeated into the fabric of Indonesian society – particularly harmful single-use plastics.

'I literally saw plastic being burnt on every other street corner,' he remembers. 'It was not only ugly and unpleasant to smell, but it was just really sad to see that's what we are doing to our planet. The way we treat the planet and the way we treat each other are closely related. That realisation was important to me.'

The BYOBottle campaign

In 2016, Berish started working for Green Music Australia, an organisation that offers support for events and musicians to become more environmentally sustainable. He was brought in to run their BYOBottle campaign, developing resources and engaging event organisers to eliminate single-use plastic water bottles from music festivals and events with the support of concerned musicians.

'Plastic water bottles didn't always exist in Australia and they weren't required to run events or festivals in the past. Thirty years later, thanks to very successful marketing, they became ubiquitous in the music industry,' Berish says.

'There was a sense that you couldn't run an event

without them. It wasn't the easiest single-use item to take on. We could have gone for straws like a lot of other groups but chose to address water bottles because it was a bigger challenge. We thought if we could achieve that, then the other items would fall into line.'

In 2017, Berish realised that they needed a specific call to action to help mobilise people on the issue. Plastic Free July 'was exactly what we needed,' he says. The BYOBottle campaign held a massive recruitment drive and engaged a new artist for each day of July. 'There were 31 new artists, which was very successful, with artists such as Jack Johnson, Paul Kelly and Missy Higgins signing up.'

To become a BYOBottle ambassador, artists had to remove single-use plastic water bottles from their drinks rider – the list of drinks they request from a venue. 'Traditionally the drinks rider included around four plastic water bottles. BYOBottle piggybacked off the energy of Plastic Free July and worked alongside it to generate enthusiasm in the music scene.'

'Let's make single-use uncool'

The BYOBottle campaign has around 40 major Australian festivals committed to eliminating bottled water and is now working with the Victorian Government's VicHealth agency to install water fountains in live music venues and seek further plastic reduction. The music artist campaign has grown to such an extent that in 2019 Jack Johnson, and a coalition of music industry leaders and environmental advocates, expanded the BYOBottle campaign internationally, launching at Byron Bay Bluesfest and recruiting artists globally including Jackson Browne, P!nk, Ben Harper and Maroon 5.

'Our approach is: let's make single-use uncool and use very influential artists as the spokespeople for this change,' Berish says. And the festival scene is a great place to implement the change. 'Festivals are very transformative and special places. People can't help but adopt a particular mindset, feeling joyous and usually quite open to receiving new ideas, not closed and confronted like the way they might be in the political arena.'

Changing festival culture

Water consumption is a crucial part of harm minimisation strategies for festivals, so taking on single-use water bottles was no small task. 'There's good reason that water consumption and hydration is a big, big deal at festivals. We deal with people's use of substances and dancing in hot environments, so tackling the issue of bottled water was taking on the status quo, on what had become the norm here in Australia,' Berish says.

Yet the campaign's uptake has been huge. 'We've managed to make serious inroads and come up with strategies in order for people to do the right thing.' Green Music Australia has also implemented reusable water-bottle hire to get all bands and festival-goers on board. 'Our rental system provides a back-up to allow people to run a strong BYOBottle-themed event. No one is getting dehydrated and we are showing that a new normal can exist.'

and insulated varieties. We kept our advice simple for people getting started: we didn't offer advice on what type of bottle was best or where to buy from; we weren't affiliated with any brands or stores and were very aware that everyone's situations and needs were different. Our focus was on encouraging people to take action and supporting a journey of change. Again the message was simple: bring your own bottle.

Number 3: The plastic straw

In 2019, US President Donald Trump's campaign manager came up with a novel idea: take thousands of bright-red plastic straws and laser-engrave them with the word 'Trump', then sell them for US$15 a pack. Reportedly the plan was born out of frustration after a paper straw he was using ripped.

For many years before that, we had been frustrated too – but for a different reason. Plastic straws were some of the most common items we collected during our beach clean-ups. This issue wasn't isolated to Australia, of course. In the same year as Trump straws were released, straws and stirrers again ranked highly in plastic litter, ranking at number three in the list of most-collected items worldwide during the International Coastal Cleanup, an initiative of the Ocean Conservancy in the US.

Although the first disposable straws were made from paper, the large-scale plastic production that started after World War II meant that it then became cheaper to manufacture straws from plastic. Plastic was more durable; it didn't go soggy and break down when immersed in liquid. These attributes led to yet another disposable plastic item being manufactured in ever-increasing numbers.

The durability and flexibility of plastic straws means they play a vital role for many people with disabilities or mobility issues. I've never doubted that a plastic single-use straw might be the best option – and sometimes the only option – for some. For most people, though, plastic straws are not used in the home, nor are they essential – yet they are frequently accepted when out and about. I've heard lots of justifications, from keeping lipstick intact through to increasing the ease of drinking milkshakes and smoothies, preventing high-speed spillage of takeaway drinks, and ensuring healthy juices don't stain lips and clothing. I've even heard people say they don't want to put their lips to a glass that has been pressed against someone else's. Yet when dining out, we accept metal cutlery, china cups and wine glasses without considering the same health implications. Plastic straws are something of an anomaly.

In some ways, plastic straws are the easiest of the Top 4 to avoid: we can politely ask for no straw in our drinks. The reality isn't always so easy, especially in the early days when it was not a common request. Sometimes busy hospitality staff forgot or ignored our pleas for a straw-free beverage, and there are still times when I get caught out because I'm just not expecting it. At a recent meeting with a waste management colleague, I asked for a glass of water with my coffee as I wanted to avoid the paper cup at the self-serve water dispenser. The glass arrived with ice and a plastic straw; I hadn't been served a plastic straw for years. Being a glass-half-full person, though, I realised that if I could add up all those straws I've avoided, they would far outweigh the few I've been given.

'I went out to dinner the other night with some friends and was the last one to order a cocktail. I asked for no straw and then everyone else ended up asking also! Even though it was only eight straws refused it still started a great conversation.'

– Alex, Plastic Free July participant

SNUB THE STRAW

Refuse plastic straws if you can, or opt for paper or reusables. Plastic Free July participants shared these tips:

- 'Make sure to request no straw when ordering.'
- 'I carry reusable straws in my handbag – easy to clean and durable.'
- 'Try natural straws such as wheat, bamboo, barley, water reed or lemongrass.'

There is an increasing number of reusable straws on the market, made from stainless steel, glass, silicone and even bamboo. Everyone seems to have their favourite type. They are lightweight and easy to carry. It comes down to preparation. It is no hassle to pop a reusable straw in your bag. Cafés, bars and restaurants are also using reusable straws more frequently, though some customers like to keep them as souvenirs. Establishments occasionally sell bamboo straws at cost to get around this.

Straws were probably the item in the Top 4 that really got people thinking the most during Plastic Free July, and the conversation has escalated over the last decade.

Number 4: The disposable cup

Trams full of commuters making their way through busy Melbourne streets are a common sight, yet one crowded tram that pulled up in the city centre on a sunny day in 2017 made people stop and stare. Instead of people, it was crammed with over 50 000 takeaway coffee cups, the number that Australians use every half-hour and throw

THE LAST STRAW

Jackie Nuñez

Founder, The Last Plastic Straw, Santa Cruz, California

Jackie Nuñez – landscaper, explorer, former river guide and now founder of The Last Plastic Straw – has seen the problems of plastic pollution firsthand. She has spent much of her life travelling and working outdoors, and has witnessed the exponential increase of plastic in the environment.

On an atoll in a World Heritage site in Belize, Jackie saw a 'river of trash' that had washed off the land after a storm. 'I became overwhelmed by the problem and when I settled down in Santa Cruz, I started doing beach clean-ups and volunteered for local organisations working on plastic pollution,' she says.

Single use, long-term damage

Jackie saw a clear disconnect between people's environmental concerns and their acceptance of single-use plastics that were 'literally in front of their noses'. 'It was like being on a boat with a hole in it, but the tap was still on,' she remembers. 'I wanted to plug up that hole and turn off the tap but I didn't know how. I was hearing about the need for behaviour change, but nothing was happening.'

In the US, 500 million straws are discarded every day. 'Most people don't realise straws don't get recycled,' she says. 'It's a wasteful item that will last for a moment in your drink but it will outlive you and generations to come in our environment.'

One day, looking out over the Monterey Bay Marine Sanctuary, just off the Californian coast, Jackie asked for a glass of water with no straw. When the attendant served her drink with a blue plastic straw sticking out of it, Jackie had her 'last plastic straw moment'. 'I thought, "Something's got to give."'

The Last Plastic Straw

The Last Plastic Straw is a movement to eliminate single-use plastic at its source. The idea emerged at the same time as Plastic Free July, when 'no one was really talking about straws'.

Jackie knew that restaurants were key to the initiative. 'If the least a restaurant could do was serve straws upon request, that's nothing off their back. It's actually asking them to do *less*. It'd be one less thing they have to buy.'

'I knew that it would be powerful. I saw the reactions of my friends. Even after beach clean-ups, we would go out for something to drink and people would be sucking on straws, and I was like, "Did you not just see what we picked up?" I saw their reactions. They were like, "Oh my gosh, I never thought about it."'

'I've bar-tended and waitressed. I know the power of suggestion ... If you say, "Would anyone like a straw?" it's hard to say no to that. A lot of people accept it whether they think about it or not. But if you change it to a *need* – "Does anyone need a straw?" – it puts the onus back on the customer. "No, actually I don't, thank you for asking" is usually the response.' She has found that up to 90 per cent of people won't ask for a straw if you don't give it to them automatically.

The sea turtle's plight

The impact of plastic waste on turtles became the last straw for many people. In August 2015, a video of a sea turtle in Costa Rica with a straw wedged in its nose went viral. It showed turtle researchers removing the straw, a procedure that took almost ten painful minutes.

'That really blew up the whole thing, even my campaign,' Jackie says. 'For a lot of people that was their last plastic straw moment and that's what it took to see the literal effect one straw could have on wildlife.'

The discussion around the video was a great way to promote Plastic Free July, and to encourage restaurants to make a difference by only offering straws upon request. 'I created this poster,' Jackie says. 'It had the cute little colourful turtle logo on there and it said, "In support of Plastic Free July we are only offering straws upon request now. Thank you for your participation. The Management." It was a great way for them to try it. It was really non-threatening.'

Straws are an entry point for change; Jackie calls her approach 'speaking truth to plastic'. 'I always encourage people, when we talk about the issue, to not get lazy and just talk about straws or cups, or whatever. It's not about the item, it's about the material. The item is what it's moulded into, but it's plastic for single use that is the problem. Plastic never was and never will be disposable, so I won't call it 'disposable' plastic. It's single use and we need to eliminate it.'

away. The sequence was filmed for the hit ABC TV series *War on Waste*, and on board the tram (the 'Bring Your Own Coffee Cup Express') was series presenter Craig Reucassel. He broadcast these figures, via megaphone and the tram's public-address system, to crowds of onlookers, dispelling the commonly held myth that the disposable cups could be recycled. 'Wake up, Melbourne, and smell the coffee,' he called out. 'Remember to bring your own coffee cup. These all end up in landfill.' A tram-load of disposable coffee cups sent to landfill every half-hour adds up to the estimated one billion cups we use each year in Australia.

It certainly got people talking. Even though the takeaway coffee cups used in Australia are mostly made from paper, they are lined with a thin coating of plastic to hold in liquids. Despite being technically recyclable in the right facility, they typically aren't since they are contaminated with coffee and have no recycling value. Many are tossed into public bins and inevitably end up as landfill.

The lids are a problem too. Despite the numbered recycling symbol, they are also destined for landfill. Some don't even make it that far; the familiar black and white discs often end up as street or pathway litter.

Disposable coffee culture

In the early 20th century the first disposable cup made from paper was invented to replace shared cups made from ceramic, metal or wood available at public water supplies. They became the cup of

> 'Takeaway is a convenience that we take for granted nowadays, because we don't immediately see the costs that it generates to society and the environment.'
>
> – Flavia Pardini, founder, 'Bring One, Get One Tree'

choice after the Spanish influenza epidemic killed millions – the health risks of shared cups were very real. The disposable cup evolved over time, with handles and plastic linings added for coffee drinkers. Some companies manufactured the cups out of polystyrene – the plastic often referred to as 'foam' – to insulate the drink and maintain its temperature. The addition of plastic lids reduced spills and allowed customers to be mobile.

We have a well-developed coffee-drinking culture in Australia too, but we don't always have time to sit and smell the coffee beans. Single-use cups increased dramatically to facilitate a grab-and-go lifestyle. Purchasing takeaway barista-brewed coffee from franchises and specialty shops is part of our social fabric in the same way that smoking cigarettes was a few decades ago.

Specially designed reusable cups for barista-style coffee have only started to enter the market in the last decade. Until then, the only options were fairly utilitarian camping and travel cups. In my camping kit at home we have a couple of insulated travel cups that worked well, a little too well – a hot cuppa would still burn your mouth half an hour after it was made.

Even though any kitchen mug will do, people's reusable cup choices have become an extension of their identity, from stainless steel 'tradie' thermoses, to stylish pottery cups that people are happy to keep in the workplace or take to their local café. The shift wasn't just about reducing waste. The cups became a talking point and a way to share solutions. Plastic Free July participants often shared photos of their cups on social media and tagged cafés to thank them. It was a seemingly small lifestyle change but one that really caught on and captured people's desire to change.

•

CUP CONTROL

Bring your reusable cup for takeaway drinks, or take the time to enjoy the sit-down café experience. Plastic Free July participants have these suggestions:

- 'I love the kitchen mug ... you don't have to be fancy with your cup.'
- 'I have a cup at work and one in my car.'
- 'I have a little reminder sticker on the front door.'
- 'We buy quality coffee beans and make our own very good coffee and take it with us.'

I doubt the inventors of the Top 4 single-use plastic items could have imagined the magnitude of their mass production and use in the decades to follow. Back in 2013, we couldn't have imagined how many people would take action to reduce the impact of these four items, nor the positive flow-on effect from individuals into their communities. It helped people to not only visualise the plastic problem but gave them an easy place to start to be part of the solution. As more and more people took this idea on board, these four small changes added up to have a big impact.

WOULD YOU LIKE A TREE WITH THAT?

Flavia Pardini

Organiser, Bring One, Get One Tree, Perth

When Flavia Pardini moved from Brazil to Perth, a career change from journalist to café manager opened her eyes to the amount of waste we create daily. She was determined to make a difference.

Waking up to the waste

Flavia had been a journalist reporting on environmental issues in Brazil and the US, so when she relocated to Perth she immediately noticed the lack of sustainability programs in her new hometown.

'I was a bit shocked with the culture here,' she recalls. 'Back then, there was very little exposure of sustainability initiatives. Waste seemed to me the tip of the iceberg, a way to get people more interested in deeper issues in a state that lived off mining and used water as if there was no tomorrow.'

Flavia had done the Earth Carers course and wanted to bring her beliefs around sustainability into her workplace. She managed the Antz Inya Pantz café in the inner-Perth suburb of Victoria Park, which has one of the longest café strips in Australia. Tackling disposable coffee cups in cafés was a good place to start.

Sharing the challenge

In 2014, Flavia introduced 'Bring One, Get One Tree', one of our Plastic Free July initiatives – via the Vic Park Collective, a volunteer group that brings the local business and resident communities together in cultural, environmental and other projects. Takeaway coffee cups weren't generally seen as a waste issue at that time, so we had a twist on the idea of 'buy one, get one free' to inspire change. For every takeaway coffee sold using the customer's reusable cup, the café recorded it and the Vic Park Collective later planted one native tree in the Victoria Park area.

The initiative was rolled out to 13 cafés, using Plastic Free July resources and adapting our promotional poster with a photo of a person holding their reusable cup in a Victoria Park setting. 'It was such a win–win as we got the council to donate native plants for each time someone showed up at the counter with a reusable cup,' Flavia says. 'We ended up with 2900 plants in the ground adjacent to Kensington Bushland … one of the few areas of bushland left in inner-city Perth.'

The concept of encouraging reusable cups grew wings. 'It started to be the normal thing to do … I like to think that "Bring One, Get One Tree" was the start of the reusable culture around cafés in Vic Park.'

One small step

'It's something very tangible and visible a coffee shop can do,' Flavia says. 'Also, at the café where I worked I was doing the ordering of disposable cups and lids and seeing the amount of money that went into buying something that was going to be used for exactly five minutes (not to mention the transport and packaging of those products).'

'Antz was also very much a place where people would linger, meet others and mix with the community, so for me it made sense to encourage people to take the time and enjoy their coffee in a "dine-in" cup. It is really a superior experience.'

The disposable cup is just one item cafés can change, creating a new mindset for other cafés and customers. Eventually the business opened Antz HQ in 2016, which was reported to be the first café in the state to go 'disposable cup–free'.

Today ...

When I visited in spring 2019, that Antz HQ café had saved 7268 disposable cups during the previous month alone. The mid-morning coffee rush hour was underway. There were labourers, office workers and yoga enthusiasts, and each had their own style of reusable cup – from 'blokey' thermoses to stylish ceramic.

In the previous three years, the Antz HQ cafe had saved 221 578 disposable cups from landfill.

5
Plastic sea

On a forest floor a fledgling flesh-footed shearwater lies near its burrow. These migratory seabirds nest on offshore islands, digging burrows to safely lay their eggs and rear their young. The chicks don't leave their nest in search of food; they wait for it to come to them. Their parents fly away from the island and hover over the ocean, swooping down to its surface to forage, typically for small fish and squid, before returning to the island to feed their chicks.

The delicate outline of the fledgling's fragile bones are in stark contrast to what lies within. In their search for food, its parents had unwittingly scooped up an assortment of brightly coloured plastic fragments before returning to the nest to feed their chicks. The shearwater's fragile rib cage had formed its own peculiar nest lined with recognisable items such as pen lids, balloon ties and bottle caps, and an assortment of plastic fragments.

Seeing these images of dead shearwater chicks for the first time truly shocked me. It's not that I didn't know about plastics harming wildlife – I'd seen pictures of seals and turtles entangled in fishing nets before – but this was so close to home, and these were items I recognised and had used in my daily life. The issue wasn't confined to some distant shore or a polluted beach in a country without waste management systems. It was happening on Lord Howe Island, a pristine World Heritage–listed paradise in the Tasman Sea between Australia and New Zealand.

The other observation that really struck me was how the shearwaters' behaviour was similar to our own. Although we aren't putting pieces of plastic into the mouths of our offspring, there is an uncomfortable parallel. As consumers we bring a miscellany of single-use plastic into our homes. These are purchasing decisions that take just moments but they have far-reaching health consequences for our planet and ourselves. Unlike the shearwaters, we do know the difference.

When I saw these images the Plastic Free July challenge was in its infancy, barely a year old. Seeing plastic in a young bird's stomach just off the coast of Australia strengthened my resolve. I wanted to learn more. How was this plastic getting into the ocean in the first place? What happened to it? This shearwater was so young that it hadn't ever left its home and our waste was being brought to it. It could have been my plastic. I felt that every piece I was able to refuse was one less piece of plastic that could potentially end up in the ocean. This was where my journey to more fully understand the plastic pollution problem began in earnest.

Diving in

Debris in the oceans isn't a recent occurrence. Driftwood washing down rivers, across oceans and onto beaches has provided coastal communities with valuable sources of timber for centuries for kindling, tools and even kayaks. With the advent of synthetic materials, the term 'marine debris' was introduced to refer to any persistent, human-created solid waste deliberately or accidentally released into the ocean. In times gone by this wasn't all bad – there was often value and even treasure in marine debris, as in the case of shipwrecks. More recently, though, the ceaseless production of synthetic materials has outpaced waste management infrastructure, resulting in leaks from the system.

The ocean and its shorelines can be deceptive. Gazing out at a blue expanse of sea, it can be hard to reconcile such breathtaking beauty with the plastic that now exists as part of the marine environment. Despite always picking up litter on my daily shoreline walks, I'd never really thought about what I'd been collecting until in 2012 I joined a group of scientists and teachers on a week-long marine debris research expedition on North Stradbroke Island in Queensland. In a forensic exercise, we set up survey lines and grids and systematically recorded each item of litter according to its material type. Later, in the laboratory, we learned how to classify them. This systematic approach revealed there was far more litter on beaches than I'd ever previously noticed, and the majority of it was plastics. As we sorted each piece into different size categories, the scores of plastic fragments became obvious, and the smaller the fragments, the more we found.

Our efforts were part of a national research project conducted by scientists at the Commonwealth Scientific and Industrial Research Organisation (CSIRO) who were surveying coastal sites every 100 kilometres around the continent of Australia, including Tasmania. It was the first continent-wide collection of rigorous scientific data undertaken anywhere in the world, and some of the results surprised me.

Dr Denise Hardesty, research scientist with CSIRO's Oceans and Atmosphere division, was one of the leaders that week. Seeing her interview on the ABC's documentary series *Catalyst* about the Lord Howe Island shearwaters had had a profound effect on me, so I was honoured to be learning from her on the expedition. She confirmed that a large proportion of the debris in our survey was plastic – and also that it was *our* plastic. 'We found that approximately

> 'Everybody thinks "It's not us" and says, "We're so clean. It's not me. It's from somewhere else." But really, when you look at [marine debris], aside from a few remote places where we get a lot of fishing gear, most of it is local in origin.'
>
> – Dr Denise Hardesty, CSIRO research scientist

three-quarters of the rubbish along the coast was plastic. Most was from Australian sources, not overseas, and the debris was concentrated near urban areas,' Denise explains. 'The heartening thing about that is that means that the solutions are close to home.'

What I learned that week confirmed that our Plastic Free July efforts were important, because many of the plastics we found on the beaches – food packaging, bags, water bottles, balloons and cups – were the same ones we used in our everyday lives. As we started to understand the top litter items and the ones that most impacted wildlife, it helped us to prioritise items to target in our Plastic Free July campaigning. I also started to observe that while people had a growing awareness of the problem and everyone who saw it felt concerned, that didn't necessarily translate into changing their behaviour to avoid those commonly littered items. I became increasingly convinced of how vital the 'reduce' message was. I saw the power of research: it would help us understand the problem so we could focus our efforts on practical solutions.

Where the water flows

The full extent of the issue has since been quantified: an astonishing 8 million metric tonnes of plastic is estimated to enter the world's oceans annually, the majority from land-based sources. Imagine five plastic shopping bags filled with plastic waste lying on every

30 centimetres of coastline around the world – that is what this amount would look like.

When I think about this devastation to our oceans, my thoughts return to my first job out of university when I was working for the government agency managing rivers and estuaries in the south-west of Western Australia. My role was to map the catchments – the areas of land where water is collected by the landscape and flows into those systems. This involved some detective work through collating maps to observe the area's topography, and reviewing studies and stormwater drainage plans.

When rain falls on land, some is absorbed but the rest flows downhill into smaller streams; these join together to form rivers that flow to the ocean. Identifying and mapping these catchment areas provided valuable information for waterways management. If we had a problem in the river such as an algal bloom, for example, we knew that it was likely to be linked to excessive fertiliser use in the catchment, and therefore where to focus our response. The images of those catchments and the flow of water stayed with me.

That same flow applies to the movement of marine debris – or litter, or pollution, as I prefer to call it, since 'debris' still conjures up images of driftwood – that primarily has land-based origins. If I pick up a mint wrapper on a beach in Fremantle, it hasn't necessarily been littered by a thoughtless patron of a local restaurant – it could have easily started its journey in Perth's CBD, some 20 kilometres upstream in the catchment. It's a chain of events that's replicated by countless people every day. Let's say a Perth office worker grabs a plastic-wrapped mint from the reception desk and unwraps it as they travel down to ground level in the lift. Heading along St Georges Terrace, they toss the wrapper in a bin, but its voyage to landfill is intercepted by a gust of wind; it takes flight and lands on the footpath. That evening, a downpour washes the wrapper into the drain and it floats to a new destination in the river. Some weeks later this thoughtfully-disposed-of single-use plastic wrapper has entered the ocean and washed up on my beach. For me it's really important to understand this pathway in order to understand the problem; it's too easy to just blame the problem on 'people who intentionally litter' rather than understanding the underlying problem of the material itself and the way we use it.

Because most plastic comes from land-based sources, understanding those sources and the ways litter travels is critical. Rivers are the potential major transport pathway for plastics into the ocean. In 2017, a group of researchers studied plastic emissions in the world's oceans via rivers by estimating the amount of plastic waste in 1350 rivers. They found the ten most polluted rivers (eight in Asia and two in Africa) account for around 90 per cent of the total plastic load entering the oceans via rivers. These rivers are in areas with populations in the hundreds of millions. Large amounts of waste in these catchments result in comparably large levels of plastic in rivers and ultimately this plastic flows out to sea. Once in the ocean, objects can float for years carried by currents and eddies. In 1992 a container ship en route from China to Seattle lost more than 28 000 rubber ducks in the Pacific. The ducks spent over a decade floating the world's oceans, some ending up on beaches as far away as Europe.

I'm often the first one in a group to notice unusual beach litter. My eyes now habitually focus at my feet rather than the horizon as I pick over the shoreline. More often than not those finds are plastic, though once on a camping holiday in the south-west corner of Western Australia my friend Damien spotted a cannonball-sized metal fishing float. The 'Made in Spain – La Coruña' marking suggested its origins and I looked at this marine artefact in amazement, contemplating its long, meandering journey to our shores. Debris in the ocean knows no boundaries.

When people litter

Though plastic pollution comes from a range of sources, intentional littering plays a role too. The reasons behind it are complex and can be situational or random. There are people who put an empty drink can in the bin, but will throw a cigarette butt onto the ground, for example, possibly thinking the butt will break down. Cigarette butts are one of the most common litter items worldwide. Apart from being toxic and unsightly, the filters aren't just paper but contain cellulose acetate, a form of plastic that will persist in the environment. I've seen people stacking their rubbish neatly around a full public beachside bin when there is an empty one just 20 metres away. I remember having a picnic on a riverbank in a small town. It was a picturesque spot where people regularly came to eat their lunch, presumably to enjoy the view. Fast-food packaging and empty drink containers littered the embankment. People are more likely to litter if there is already rubbish on the ground; there is a sort of herd mentality around it. Many people who leave their rubbish behind at festivals or in cinemas would never dream of repeating that behaviour in a different context, and unfortunately it goes back to the idea that someone else will deal with it.

Education campaigns to reduce littering behaviour are important and have had varying levels of success, yet litter, regardless of our intent, can end up in rivers and ultimately our oceans. The lightweight nature of plastic means it can easily be swept up by the wind or washed into waterways when it escapes from an overfilled bin or a crowded event space. Balloon releases – ceremonial events where people gather and unleash large numbers of hydrogen- or helium-filled balloons to mark special occasions – are a classic example of unintentional littering. What goes up must eventually come down, and where this litter will fall is anyone's guess. In 2017, three balloons were found on a beach on Lord Howe Island. The bright red

'For my daughter's birthdays we spend time together on the night before her party making a big "Party" sign for the front door instead of balloons – she loves doing this. We have special decorations we get out every year (bunting, candles) rather than balloons – these things are family treasures.'

– Jen, Plastic Free July participant

background and gold logo identified their starting point as a festival in Sydney some 800 kilometres to the south-west.

Litter doesn't just affect the environment. It also has diverse impacts across economies, safety and health. In water it can pose a boating hazard – propellers can become entangled in fishing net and ropes, and lost shipping containers pose a real risk to watercraft. Polluted beaches negatively affect tourism, water sitting in littered plastic containers in tropical environments can become breeding grounds for disease-carrying mosquitoes, and plastic can transport invasive species across oceans. One of our Earth Carers, Amina Syed, told me about the problem of littered plastic bags she encountered back in her home city of Lahore, Pakistan. Just before the arrival of monsoon rains, the city's waste management company sends over 100 crews of workers to clear blocked drains of waste to prevent flooding or disease from stagnating water. Plastic bags are a particular problem as they become tangled in tree branches and other waste, forming dam-like structures.

While working in local government I visited many waste facilities and witnessed how much effort goes into preventing waste escaping and becoming litter. Waste sites are frequently swept, and litter fences are placed strategically around the perimeter of the sites. These are costly exercises, especially considering the size of waste facilities and the hundreds of thousands of tonnes of waste they process each year. Plastic at these sites was always the main problem, plastic bags in particular – they became snagged on the litter fences and waved in the breeze like prayer flags.

Tiny pieces, big problem

Many people who take on the Plastic Free July challenge are concerned about how long it takes for plastic to break down. The reality is, unlike organic material such as paper, food scraps or plant matter, plastic doesn't break *down*. In the environment, when it's exposed to sunlight and the elements, it instead breaks *up* into smaller and smaller pieces. It is important to understand this. We cannot look at the fate of plastics in the environment in the same way as we would consider an apple core being thrown into the garden or a littered paper bag.

Responses to the question 'How long does a plastic bag take to break down?' vary greatly. I've seen estimates that range from ten years to a thousand years. But do we really know? Plastic bags were invented just under 50 years ago, so technically we can't yet know what state they will be in as landfill or litter in years to come. But if we only concern ourselves with how long plastic takes to 'break down', we are sending the wrong message. Instead, we must consider what happens to those pieces of plastic, where they end up and what their impacts are. Plastic bags are used on average for 12 minutes before they are disposed of. *This* is what I think we need to focus on.

As with cigarette butts, wet wipes are another example of an item thought to be 'biodegradable', so people don't actually consider leaving them in the environment as littering. Wet wipes aren't a paper tissue but are made from typically plastic fibres, often polyester. Frequently marketed as 'flushable' they can end up blocking sewers (creating giant 'fatbergs' in wastewater systems), or they can end up in the environment. In a clean-up of a small section of the banks of the River Thames in London in 2019, a staggering 4000 wet wipes were collected in one 400-metre stretch. I've also encountered them on the side of hiking tracks in remote areas. Unfortunately, when nature called, these hikers didn't think about the effect of their litter on the environment.

Microplastics

The visible nature of plastic makes it easy to identify, but some plastics are insidious, finding their way into marine environments in a stealth-like manner that enhances their reach and increases their harmful effects. Microplastics are very small plastic pieces less than 5 millimetres long that come from a variety of sources. Some are fragments degraded from once larger pieces, but others have different origins.

Plastic microbeads are tiny pieces of plastic used for exfoliating and scrubbing that are added to a range of products, including personal care, cosmetics and cleaning products. These synthetic beads replaced natural materials such as apricot kernels, ground pumice or silica. A single product can contain hundreds of thousands of microbeads, and since they are cheap, they are also used as fillers or emulsifying agents. The facial scrub with 'energising microbeads' offering a 'tingly cool lather' that once appealed to my daughter, and the blue flecks found in some toothpastes, are in fact made of plastic. Once people woke up to the fact that microbeads were made from plastics such as polyethylene and nylon they were rightfully outraged. Some countries have banned microbeads and some businesses have stopped using them of their own accord. In Australia, a ban has not yet been implemented and instead a voluntary phase-out is in place. It is up to individuals to read the ingredients lists on personal care and household cleaning products and find alternatives without microbeads.

Another significant source of microplastics is plastic microfibres – very small thread-like fibres released when we wash synthetic clothing and other household textiles. Increasingly clothing is made using plastic textiles such nylon and polyester. Outdoor wear such as polar fleeces made from recycled plastic bottles also releases microfibres.

Plastic microbeads and microfibres flow straight from our household drains into waste-water systems. Domestic washing machines and wastewater treatment plants aren't designed to filter out such small particles, so they enter the environment and ultimately oceans. Other microplastic sources include car tyres, fishing gear, synthetic ropes, tarpaulins … the list goes on. The more we use plastic, the more it is released into the environment. And it is not just wildlife being impacted; it is ending up back in our bodies, identified in our food by an ever-increasing number of studies. Microplastics have been found in seafood, sea salt, honey, beer, chicken, water, tea bags, bottled water and, as a result, in our faeces. The question should probably now be 'Where *isn't* it?'

FIRST STEPS YOU CAN TAKE TO REDUCE OCEAN PLASTIC

1. Simply refuse single-use plastic. Think of it as a gimmick that has reached its use-by date.
2. Join in on an organised clean-up or Take 3 For The Sea (see the box 'Buoyed by Hope' on page 104) and do your own collection whenever you are outdoors. Get kids in on the act too.
3. Watch a documentary such as *Bag It* or *A Plastic Ocean*, or a series like *Blue Planet II* to learn more about the plastic problem, or organise a community screening to start a conversation.

Close to home

When a member of our Plastic Free July group discovered microplastic pollution at nearby Minim Cove in Perth, it really localised the problem for us and provided a talking point to get local engagement. Our team went down to the river to see for ourselves. My colleague Amy Warne recalled how serious it was. 'I remember thinking, "We just can't clean it up. We have to reduce it."'

Minim Cove is a leafy green development in one of Perth's more affluent areas on the banks of the Swan River, just a few kilometres upriver from Fremantle Harbour. Trapped in the reeds on the riverbank below manicured parks and multimillion-dollar houses was what could only be described as plastic soup. Like hundreds and thousands on fairy bread, there was quite literally hundreds and thousands of plastic pieces, mostly broken-down fragments, in every colour of the rainbow. It was improbable this litter just came from this suburb; it was more likely a mixing zone, trapping plastics that wash downstream via the river from the whole catchment of the city of Perth, as well as travelling in from the ocean.

We scooped up a sample in a big glass jar and preserved it with ethyl alcohol. Among small pieces of reeds, the jar was full of small pieces of plastic including plastic caps, fragments of packaging, polystyrene foam, pieces of rope, lollipop sticks, small toys, a numbered ear-tag from a sheep and thousands of 'nurdles' – also called 'mermaid's tears' – the pearl-sized plastic resin pellets that are the raw material from the plastics production process.

I think what shocked us was that this was in our own backyard, at a place that we were deeply connected to. We had only seen pictures like this in movies. In Australia, where we have sophisticated waste management systems and litter prevention programs, the plastics explosion was still happening. The littering wasn't necessarily intentional, but that didn't prevent the end result. That jar was like a plastic pollution snow dome – a microcosm of the plastic infecting our waterways. It travelled with us when we gave community talks, and we passed it around to school students and displayed it at local events. No one ever could guess that we had scooped up that much plastic from the nearby Swan River.

The sight of so many nurdles was mind boggling. These resin pellets hadn't even been manufactured into a product and yet they were still causing pollution. They were in pristine condition, too, so it was likely that they were coming from a factory upstream making items such as buckets or kayaks or containers from this plastic. They were so small and light and there was so many of them. Somehow they had been washed or blown 'away'. But again, 'away' isn't nowhere. We were encountering that place. It was a grim realisation.

The 'Great Pacific Garbage Patch'

When boat captain Charles Moore sailed from Hawaii to southern California in 1997, his vessel was becalmed and spent several days motoring across the 'eerily still waters of the mid-Pacific doldrums'. Some 1600 kilometres from land, each day Moore noticed shards of plastic on the ocean's surface. He wrote about the extent of the garbage and, while he maintains what he and his crew had found was not an 'island of trash' but rather a 'thin plastic soup', it became popularised as the 'Great Pacific Garbage Patch', a phenomenon claimed by some to be 'as big as the state of Texas' – almost 700 000 square kilometres. Though the names vary, what isn't disputed is that it is a major plastic accumulation zone in the North Pacific Gyre.

I had read Charles Moore's book *Plastic Ocean*, which describes that voyage and the work he has done since, and I was really keen to see the problem firsthand. Several years later, I jumped at the opportunity to join an expedition researching plastic pollution in the North Atlantic Ocean where scientists were studying microplastics.

Despite my lack of sailing experience, in 2014 I joined the 72-foot yacht *Sea Dragon* as a crew member on a two-week voyage from Cornwall in south-west England to the Azores in the North Atlantic Ocean, west of continental Portugal. Spending that long being disconnected from the modern world and without seeing land was a refreshing break and an opportunity to connect with nature. We encountered seabirds and marine mammals around the vessel and gazed up at the sky from sunrise to sunset with uninterrupted horizons. One day a school of around 1000 Atlantic white-sided dolphins accompanied *Sea Dragon* as it sailed south. Far from my visions of encountering floating islands of plastic, the ocean seemed clean – the odd plastic bag, bottle and fishing buoy here and there, mostly when close to shore, but days would go by without anything unnatural appearing on the surface.

Getting up close revealed a different story. Every day, at 2 pm, the crew attached a net from the boom and towed it alongside the boat for 20 minutes, sieving the water and collecting particles from the surface. The resulting catch was analysed and separated into organic debris, marine organisms and plastic particles. As the appointed official recorder, I sat on deck every day to note details such as the time the net was deployed and retrieved, and the weather conditions. During those 20-minute surveys I never saw any plastics floating on the surface, yet every single sample collected contained plastics, including fragments, film, fibres from rope, a barcode sticker and even nurdles. Even though the North Atlantic Gyre has lower concentrations of plastic than the North Pacific, we were seeing the 'plastic soup' that Charles Moore referred to. Although I don't work as a scientist or consider myself an expert, experiencing the problem firsthand helped me to understand the issues and then to share those insights with people doing the Plastic Free July challenge who were really interested to learn as much as they could. It buoyed them to keep making changes in their own lives.

> 'Plastic Free July had a huge awareness-raising impact. I hadn't really thought about the ocean impacts before – it was making that link between the plastics found inside fish, for example, and what I do at home that I wasn't aware of.'
>
> – Frances, Plastic Free July participant

Surveying the plastic soup

Through the Plastic Free July challenge, I have not only read extensively about the plastics issue, but have been privileged to meet many people at the forefront of plastics research. Hearing their stories first-hand and asking questions has been such a valuable part of my learning. Oceanographer Dr Julia Reisser was one of the first participants in Plastic Free July and her ocean pollution research starkly reinforced the need to keep working towards removing plastic from its source. After studying plastic in marine turtles in her homeland of Brazil, where '100 per cent have ingested plastic', Julia's studies took her to Australia where she completed microplastics surveys, deploying manta trawl nets – nets shaped like manta rays that collect samples from the ocean's surface – from boats around the coastline. She confessed that she didn't realise how big the problem was in 'clean places like Australia'. When she started her research around eight years ago, people weren't making the connection between plastic consumption and marine debris research.

Julia continued her mission, relocating to the Netherlands to join The Ocean Cleanup as chief scientist with the formidable task of mapping the 'Great Pacific Garbage Patch'. In 2015, the team began the largest ocean research expedition ever undertaken, deploying 30 boats to sail between Hawaii and California and following up with an aerial expedition to map large debris. This allowed the researchers to quantify larger items such as discarded fishing nets – 'ghost nets'

– that they had not previously been able to capture in their analysis from boats.

'I really got a grasp of what it looks like,' says Julia. 'It's beautiful blue ocean there, but then sometimes you get strips or fronts, and then it's just depressing, because you have lots of plastic in different sizes. I think it looks like confetti but it's actually made of objects like buoys and ghost nets.' The plastic formed hotspots, or accumulation zones. From the air Julia also observed marine mammals, including a baby sperm whale, at the surface of the garbage patch.

The Ocean Cleanup has since been working on designing river clean-up systems, focusing on South-East Asia. 'What we found out is that if you stop the flow of river plastic from a few rivers, you can already make a big difference in terms of mitigation.'

What animals endure

There was one number that really got people talking. In 2016, a report called the *New Plastics Economy*, published by the World Economic Forum and the Ellen MacArthur Foundation, predicted that if 'business as usual' continued with the current systems of plastics use and disposal, by the year 2050 plastic waste would outweigh fish in the world's oceans. Trying to grasp that scenario is staggering, but we can't deny the plastic that is already in our oceans and washed up on our shores – and we can't deny its source. A dead whale's body spills plastic bags; a turtle is entangled in a fishing net; a hermit crab uses a bottle cap as its shell. It is *our* plastic.

Images of wildlife being impacted by plastics have become disturbingly frequent in the media. Marine organisms are affected by plastic pollution mostly by becoming entangled in it or ingesting it. Consumption of plastic debris also exposes organisms to contamination from toxic chemicals; these may have been added to the plastics

HIGH-RISK PLASTIC

Commonly littered items that pose a high risk to marine wildlife include:

- fishing line and ropes
- plastic bags
- balloons
- plastic food packaging
- straws and stirrers
- plastic utensils.

during production or absorbed from pollution in the water. It is not just an oceans issue either – on the banks of the Ganges in India, watching the nightly Ganga ritual worshipping the river, I noticed a cow on the edge of the ceremony chewing a plastic bag it had retrieved from the litter-strewn ground.

As plastics break up into smaller and smaller pieces they are distributed around the ocean, from the surface to the deepest ocean trenches, and from the equator to the polar ice caps. The impact of microplastics in the oceans extends to organisms at the base of the marine food web, with mussels, worms and even tiny zooplankton ingesting them.

Plastic litter has had the most impact in areas with diverse wildlife, even where waters are relatively pristine. Denise Hardesty from the CSIRO explained the findings of their marine debris research close to home: 'Plastics may have the greatest impact on wildlife where they gather in the Southern Ocean, in a band around the southern edges of Australia, South Africa and South America. This is largely because of the number and diversity of seabirds who pass through these waters – it isn't that the waters are dirtier here per se, it's more that there is immense biodiversity in the region, so it's a higher risk area here.'

Seabirds in crisis

I could not have envisaged that my 'I'm going plastic free next month' revelation would have taken me on this journey so full of new knowledge and valuable experiences. Each one reinforced how important waste avoidance was, and the role that Plastic Free July could play. Meeting incredibly passionate people from around the world who were working to address the issue of plastic pollution guided my understanding and helped grow the challenge. After watching the footage of the flesh-footed shearwater chicks on Lord Howe Island, I eventually got to meet Dr Jennifer Lavers, the featured research scientist working on that population. As I sat with her outside a café just down the road from my home, bombarding her with questions, I still couldn't comprehend any bird having plastic in its stomach.

'The most I ever found in a single chick was 276 pieces of plastic,' Jennifer told me. This was in 2011, when she had only been travelling to Lord Howe Island for about five years, and was still relatively new to the issue. 'My colleague Dr Ian Hutton and I were at the research station, nothing fancy, and we didn't really know what was going to come out of that bird, but I could feel from holding its body that this was going to be something different.'

The necropsy was filmed. Jennifer had to fight back tears. 'I was speaking to the camera and trying to just document what I was seeing in a factual way, but on the inside, my brain and my heart were exploding. I remember just sitting there after the camera was turned off, blinking and shaking in utter disbelief.' The plastic weighed 64 grams, which was about 14 per cent of the bird's body mass. For the average person that would be like having somewhere between 10 and 12 kilograms of plastic in their stomach.

'It was a pivotal, transformational moment in my life that shaped me,' Jennifer says. 'I'm a different person now. That bird means something … it was just one animal but it changed my life in a moment. I sat there thinking that this animal's parents, lovingly, unknowingly, accidentally fed it to death. I thought, *What have we done? And how do we share this with the world?* My work is to give a voice to the voiceless and I feel like our wildlife is voiceless.'

I couldn't imagine what that would feel like – having 10 to 12 kilos of plastic in my stomach. Would I still even feel hungry? What damage would those sharp fragments cause when they pressed against the bird's stomach?

In 2016, I received a Churchill Fellowship which provided me with an opportunity to explore the problem internationally. Established 50 years ago, after the death of Sir Winston Churchill, the Fellowships support Australians to travel overseas to research inspiring practices that will in turn benefit Australian communities.

My journey first led me to Hawaii in the North Pacific Ocean, where plastic pollution has been observed and studied for decades. I visited the seaside laboratory of scientists Michelle Hester and David Hyrenbach to learn more about the impact of plastics on seabirds. Upon arrival they presented me with a traditional Hawaiian greeting gift of a lei, which they placed over my head.

Like the flesh-footed shearwaters on Lord Howe Island, the albatrosses they study fly long distances across oceans in search of food floating on the surface. Because of this behaviour, the stomach contents of seabirds tells the story of what's on the surface of our oceans. Adult birds return to their nesting grounds and regurgitate their stomach contents directly into the mouths of chicks. After five or six months, as the chicks prepare to leave their nests for the first time, the young birds regurgitate all the non-digestible material from their stomachs in a mass known as a bolus. Unfortunately, among organic materials such as squid beaks, pumice stones and fish bones, nearly all boluses from albatrosses now contain plastic.

Feeling the physical weight of plastic that had been in and out of the stomachs of two seabirds in my hands was distressing. It was a disturbing array of recognisable items including fishing line, bottle caps, children's toys and even a cigarette lighter. Leaving the meeting, I headed north up to the east coast of Oahu, a dramatically beautiful landscape where deep-green forested mountains meet the sea. The contrast between this immense beauty, the laboratory discussions and the harrowing images in my head caused me to pull off to the side of the road and start to weep. The lei around my neck was made from plastic Michelle and David had collected from one albatross bolus and it weighed heavily upon me.

It's now up to humans

Encountering the enduring legacy of our plastic waste has had a profound impact on me. While I was learning about the devastating effects of plastic on our wildlife, I met with artist Chris Jordan, who has spent years capturing images of the Laysan albatross, on Midway Atoll in the North Pacific, that have been impacted by plastic. The images portraying dead albatrosses with plastic-filled stomachs are both shocking and powerful. He wanted to tell the story of the 'Great Pacific Garbage Patch', but because the problem is so widespread he instead focused on capturing the story through individual birds. Chris took these photos, he says, as a way of 'reflecting back to us our broken relationship with the living world in this incredibly iconic way'.

Though facing the ramifications of our waste can be incredibly challenging, ignoring the issue simply isn't acceptable. I find that working on the Plastic Free July challenge requires a constant balance between sharing and acknowledging the devastating plastic problem, and keeping up the positive momentum that comes from people being empowered to make a difference. Chris questions how we can 'step out of our denial of our consumption and its impacts and not fall into despair'. It is a difficult question to answer. I suspect that Chris, like many of us, is driven to act because humans have created this issue, so it is humans who must address it. It falls back on us to do whatever we can, with whatever skills we have, to tread more lightly, reduce our impact and work towards repairing the damage already done.

I know I am not alone in how I feel about this problem. No one I speak to feels okay when they learn about the impacts of litter on marine wildlife. Through Plastic Free July I have had lots of opportunities to give presentations and although my approach is to focus on solutions, I do share stories of what I have seen. Though the lei made of plastic fragments is quite garish, I sometimes wear it when presenting, as much as a reminder to myself as a talking point. At the conclusion of one conference presentation, I took off the necklace, held it in my hand and shared the story of the albatross chick. Numbers can be overwhelming, and the problem feels so immense when you discuss tonnes of plastics in the ocean, numbers of species affected and recycling rates. Instead, just telling the story of one bird can challenge people to choose one thing in their own lives they can change. When I pose the question 'How much is too much in one stomach?' to an audience, it is a lasting reminder.

Mopping up the problem

Imagine if you returned home from work one afternoon to find your kitchen floor was flooded because the tap had been left on. What is the first thing you would do? Would you reach for a mop and bucket? Or would you first deal with the problem at its source and then mop up the damage? This scenario is frequently used to describe the approach we need to take to tackle the plastic pollution problem and why we have to 'turn off the tap'. Clean-ups are really just mopping the floor – but maybe, in order to alert people to the problem and become aware of the immensity of the task, we need to turn our attention to the running tap.

BUOYED BY HOPE

Tim Silverwood

Co-founder, Take 3 For The Sea, Central Coast, New South Wales

Take 3 For The Sea encourages people to play an active role in helping to reduce plastic pollution by taking three pieces of plastic when visiting beaches, waterways and other natural areas.

Tim's desire to make a difference stemmed from a surfing and backpacking pilgrimage from Bali to the Himalayas in his mid-twenties. It was a life-changing voyage. 'Every step of the way, I encountered pollution I had never really seen before and where it really culminated was at the end destination in Kashmir.

'I was in this little mountain village and each day a tractor towing a trailer would go to each guesthouse to collect waste. The end of the journey for that tractor was the side of the mountain where the waste would be dumped.' That was, as Tim puts it, 'the straw that lodged in the turtle's nose'.

'I knew my rubbish was in there. Even though I put it in the bin, it was now in the Himalayas and it was going to go all the way to the ocean.'

The message sinks in

On his return home, Tim's determination to make a difference connected him with marine ecologist Roberta Dixon-Valk and youth educator Amanda Marechal, and the Take 3 For The Sea concept took shape.

The message was simple. A deep connection to the beach extended to a connection with the rubbish that had been left behind. Noticing it was a wake-up call. Removing it made a difference. 'It was something people could adopt as part of their everyday behaviour,' Tim says.

'Take 3 For The Sea and Plastic Free July are organisations borne out of the east and west coast of Australia that have penetrated well beyond those boundaries. They get people involved in different ways.

'It's not easy and no one's perfect. Pretty much everything we do has an impact somehow on the environment, it's just not always obvious – even driving cars results in tyre abrasion, which is one of the leading contributors to microplastic pollution in the ocean.'

'We have to maintain hope'

Both Plastic Free July and Take 3 For The Sea are organisations with a common goal. Take 3 For The Sea participants join in on the Plastic Free July challenge and we encourage challengers to do Take 3 for the Sea clean-ups. Tim is adamant that the collaborative momentum needs to keep going to be a driving force for change.

The slow, steady and reasoned approach is a useful lesson. Many people who have worked on waste solutions for an extended period of time emphasise that striving for perfection or rushing to the finish line is an impossible task.

The response from young people keeps him motivated, Tim says. 'I'll be talking to an audience of students and they just get it. They say, "Yeah, let's pick up three bits of rubbish." You show them a problem and they want to find a solution.

'It is about being optimistic. We have to maintain hope. What on earth does our planet look like if we've lost hope?'

Marine plastic pollution has captured our attention but it's far more than an ocean problem. Beach clean-ups are a powerful way to raise awareness and engage the community's hearts and minds around the plastic waste issue, and data collected can be a key tool for reducing plastics at their source (i.e. turning off the tap) and holding producers accountable. Around the world, clean-up efforts have inspired and engaged community action, at the same time acknowledging the bigger picture: just cleaning up the mess isn't going to fix the problem. Each year Break Free From Plastic conducts global audits of branded litter items conducted during community clean-ups to identify and name corporate plastic polluters. In Australia, Heidi Taylor is managing director and founder of Tangaroa Blue, a not-for-profit organisation that conducts beach clean-ups and aims to stop plastic pollution at its source. 'If all we ever do is clean up, that's all we'll ever do,' Heidi says. 'The extra effort that citizen scientists take in recording data on what they have picked up means that we have evidence to be able to push for change. Without this vital data, it is difficult to influence the way individuals, businesses and government agencies operate. We see our volunteers not as rubbish collectors, but as our marine debris CSI team whose efforts are just as important as removing the rubbish in the first place.'

The situation can perhaps be likened to a parent who constantly tidies up after their child. The child gets so used to this behaviour that they continue to leave their mess for the parent to deal with. The parent can't stand looking at towels on the bed or dirty clothes on the floor, and so even though it frustrates them, they continue to clean up so they can have a tidy home. The cycle continues and no one learns anything. Personally, it would be hard for me to walk past litter – and I don't imagine this as ever being a possibility – but sometimes I wonder what would happen if one day everyone in the world just stopped picking it up. What if all the formal and informal clean-ups and street cleaning just stopped? How 'dirty' would things get? What would our streets, parks and beaches look like after a day, a week or a month? Much of the cost of cleaning up plastic pollution is borne by the community and local authorities, and the impact is borne by our environment. Who would pay that price if we didn't?

Too close to home

On 1 June 2018, the community of Port Stephens on the east coast of Australia was alerted to a shipping container spill following heavy seas. Eighty-one shipping containers went overboard from the vessel YM *Efficiency* on its route from Taiwan to Port Botany in Sydney.

Port Stephens is a popular tourist destination 200 kilometres north of Sydney, offering turquoise bays, white sand dunes, and whale and dolphin cruises. Following the container spill, recreational boaters and commercial operators were told to keep an eye out for hazards: the containers were floating beneath the surface, and associated debris had come loose, so they posed a clear navigational risk. A growing local awareness of the potential environmental impact quickly followed. People gathered at Yacaaba Head, Jimmys Beach and Hawks Nest to collect debris that had washed ashore. In a region famous for its pristine beaches and rocky outcrops, the sight of disposable nappies, sanitary items, food packaging and plastic cups was an immediate call to action.

Varley Group was the principal contractor tasked with the challenging clean-up directly following the spill. Craig Brittliffe, marine and industrial manager of Varley Group, described single-use plastics as a major component. Worse, these brand-new items didn't even end up being single use; instead they were no use.

'It was extensive – plastic lids, thousands of plastic cups, plastic cream containers, plastic lolly wrappers, styrofoam, car bumper bars, long-life milk cartons, plastic clocks, printer cartridges and car tyres,' Craig says.

'It has had a personal impact. Two-minute noodle containers have a styrofoam bowl, plastic outer seal, and inner plastic sachets containing sauces and spices. I have not bought or eaten one since working on the project. We also collected hundreds of water bottles that had nothing to do with the shipping container incident. In some areas we found more rubbish than that related to the container spill. They had been there a long time and appeared not to have broken down at all.'

Local diver Greg Finn – husband of my co-author Joanna – was engaged to assist with the clean-up. The dive team would sometimes converge at his family home to discuss the day's 'catch'.

'I'm used to diving for shellfish, but instead I was fishing for plastic – plastic wrapped around kelp stalks, waterlogged plastic nappies, delaminated single-use milk cartons, plastic bags full of black sesame powder, kilometres of shrink wrap and single-use plastic cups. *Thousands* of single-use plastic cups,' Greg remembers. 'This was at the same time that my family started our first ever Plastic Free July challenge.'

As of January 2020, 66 shipping containers from YM *Efficiency* have been identified and five have been removed. A further 15 are yet to be found. International marine services company Ardent has been tasked with removing the remaining containers and debris in 2020.

Around the world, approximately 10 000 shipping containers are lost every year.

The mounting pressure on oceans

Although most plastic pollution comes from the land, it has an increasingly damaging effect on our waterways and the living

> 'It was one thing to see plastic on the supermarket shelves, but collecting it from the sea floor really made me think about what we put in our trolley and it changed our family's buying habits.'
> – Greg Finn, diver

creatures, including ourselves, that rely on our oceans for survival. Oceans make up the largest proportion of our planet. They are the foundations of life, generating oxygen, absorbing carbon dioxide, providing food and regulating our climate.

The ocean sustains us, but it is also a lifegiver in a more nuanced sense. Many of us have an enduring relationship with our shorelines and oceans. We sit on the sand to reflect on life or escape the day's stresses, and we hurl ourselves into the sea to be rejuvenated. Casting a line off a wharf to catch a fresh fish is a rite of passage for many coast dwellers. To see these formerly pristine environments damaged by plastic is like a punch to the gut. This isn't an issue that is hidden or one that can be ignored. The effects are there for all of us to see. Of course not all marine plastic is immediately visible. Microplastics are insidious in the way they create havoc for our animals and the environment.

None of this is defendable. Nor is it sustainable. Plastic pollution is yet another pressure on oceans already threatened by a changing climate, acidification, fishing pressures and loss of habitat.

It can feel incredibly overwhelming. It is understandable to have a sense of powerlessness against a rising tide of plastic, but learning about the issue and taking action through our purchasing habits helps to drive the momentum we all need. No individual act is trivial, because those actions combined send strong messages to corporations, governments and the many people in organisations across the world who are working every day of their lives to address plastic pollution and its effect on marine environments.

What gives me hope is the increased awareness and discussion of the issue that I have seen over the last decade. As painful as seeing this problem is, raising awareness and concern can be the first step that leads to people making change. As the Plastic Free July challenge evolved we were always very motivated by the problem at a deeply personal level. Sure, we did share the issues and our learnings but the focus was on solutions. And absolutely no blame.

•

Not long after going on that trip to North Stradbroke Island I sat with my son Leeuwin looking through a photo album from a decade earlier. There was a photo of us setting off to attend a protest against a planned development at Ningaloo Reef, a World Heritage area in my state's north-west, and home to numerous marine species including turtles. We'd made hand-painted signs from recycled cardboard in the shape of turtles and one read 'Ningaloo for Turtles'. Tied to the handles of his pram when he was a two-year-old were bright green and blue balloons to draw attention to our protest.

As I looked at those images, the irony certainly wasn't lost on me. We just didn't know. But once we *did* know, we chose to do things differently. The learning curve keeps moving us along its arc and, with more information, we respond in new ways to the plastic challenge. It is dynamic, more like a series of waves, the relentless energy of many people sharing ideas in inspiring ways.

6

Try to do better

My Sunday ritual starts early, timed to beat the crowds. With a basket balanced on my forearm, I work my way through my local farmers' market. Each weekend local growers come here to sell their fresh seasonal produce, and the marquee stalls are lined with apples, oranges and leafy green vegetables.

The pace is leisurely. We've gotten to know the growers and each year I look forward to Philomena and John arriving with their mandarins and oranges, Grace and Albert's free-range eggs, and Charlie's coriander in May and tomatoes in time for Christmas. There's time to chat about where the vegetables have been grown, find out what's in season or the best way to ripen an avocado. Recipes are exchanged – new ideas to cook fennel or a favourite winter soup. After shopping it's time for a weekly catch-up with friends over coffee.

I'd always enjoyed shopping this way, but when I made my commitment to reduce single-use plastic it became a routine. I could no longer rely on convenience, because convenience almost always meant packaging. Loose, unwrapped fruit and vegetables were almost non-existent at my local supermarket. The farmers' market – along with buying pantry items in bulk, cooking more meals from scratch and taking my own containers to the delicatessen – has allowed me to significantly reduce my plastic packaging. And the experience of the market is much more personal, offering the chance to strike up conversations and exchange ideas. Sunday shopping has become a time of learning, and a social gathering that goes far beyond buying fruit and vegetables.

I live on the west coast of Australia, with desert on one side and the vast Indian Ocean on the other, in one of the most isolated major cities in the world. It has a harsh Mediterranean climate, blasted on summer mornings by hot winds from the desert and in the afternoons by a strong sea breeze coming up from the Southern Ocean. Somehow, in this arid landscape, seeds sprout and plants grow.

Strolling through the market each week, I am struck by the positive changes people make when an idea inspires them to act. Over the years, the organisers have worked with stallholders to reduce plastic as much as possible. Each week they set up wash-up stations near the coffee van with a selection of secondhand cups to borrow and return. And I've been quietly chuffed as I see the friends I meet each week start making changes too, such as bringing reusable produce bags.

Brothers Chris and Charlie Maus are growers and stallholders at the market. Over the past few years, they have reduced the plastics they use in transporting their produce, and have noticed how customers have come on board. 'The use of reusables has become much more prevalent,' Charlie notes. 'People have stopped asking for bags. It used to be that people would sometimes forget or ask out of habit, but now they bring their own. It's pretty good – people are even returning the little packaging we do use, such as punnets, for us to reuse, or the jars we sell our honey in. We encourage people to do this.'

I see the same kind of long-lasting change with Plastic Free July. Within a few years the idea had taken root. It sparked conversations and rapidly flourished. People felt good about the changes they were making, forming new habits such as shopping at farmers' markets and local independent stores, connecting with their community and seeing their bins less full. We learned about these changes through casual conversations. The movement increasingly took on a life of its own.

A challenge becomes a habit

By 2013, the third year of Plastic Free July, the challenge had become an annual ritual in our lives. It expanded from being something we 'just did' each July to a more intentional campaign. The one-month challenge was often compared to 'Dry July' and there were definite parallels – both relied on people 'going without' or finding alternatives. Refusing single-use plastic wasn't quite as straightforward as refusing alcohol (though some would beg to differ). In certain circumstances, like being offered a plastic straw at a bar, it was simply a matter of politely refusing, but in other situations, such as grocery shopping, the solutions weren't always so obvious or readily available. Finding alternatives involved research and preparation.

2013 was a tipping point and not just because of the Top 4. We became more attuned to the diverse needs of participants and the journey they were going on, as well as their growing appetite for solutions and passion to help others. With increasing numbers of people joining the challenge, there wasn't a 'one size fits all' solution to avoiding plastic. Everyone had unique needs, preferences and difficulties. It got to the point where so many people were taking part and asking questions that we didn't have the resources or people power to cope with the demand. The number of inquiries swamped our small team. People from other states would phone and ask where they could buy milk in plastic-free containers or how to make their own toothpaste.

The business development manager at the Western Metropolitan Regional Council, Rebecca Goodwin, suggested we gather and share this information in one place. I remember her putting together all our ideas, tips and recipes into a website over one weekend. That perhaps gives you a glimpse into how informal our systems were. We drew on each other's strengths and although our process was quite reactive, it worked.

'Building the website and using social media helped us to deliver the campaign by giving people resources and helping them to avoid single-use plastic,' Rebecca recalls. 'Otherwise we were being bombarded by questions via email and phone calls because there just wasn't that much information around at the time. We started collating our ideas and documenting our resources.'

Today there is an ever-growing number of plastic-free and zero-waste blogs and books available, but back in 2013 information wasn't so easy to find. Our website became a repository of ideas for alternatives to plastic that plugged the information gap. Our campaign resources were an eclectic mix of everyone's ideas, illustrated by photos from our own homes and shopping trips, our long-suffering partners and children, and even our pets. It certainly wasn't a typical education campaign with a fixed set of instructions on how to succeed at the challenge or a step-by-step guide to plastic-free perfection. The approach was simply 'here are some ideas we have found'. People could go to the website and find alternatives or a recipe that would offer them a plastic-free option.

'The whole idea was that we wanted to make it shareable. It was important to get the message out there to the average person, to all the mums and dads ... because it was just so darn hard to avoid plastic,' Rebecca says.

We kept adding new website content as our growing audience shared solutions or encountered roadblocks. Our discussions evolved as people moved beyond the obvious things like plastic bags and water bottles to trying to deal with the sheer volume of plastic in all areas of their lives; there were always lots of questions coming in. The feedback we were getting from those trying Plastic Free July

POPULAR IDEAS FOR PLASTIC-FREE LIVING

1 Choose loose products. Skip the little plastic bag, or put items in a reusable bag.
2 Look for bulk food options near you. *Zero Waste Home* (zerowastehome.com) has a 'Bulk Finder' that you can search.
3 Use reusable containers, wax wraps, or bowls covered with plates to store food in the fridge.
4 Switch from liquid soap to bar soap.
5 Food and liquids can be frozen in glass jars by leaving an inch or two of headspace. Use wide-mouthed jars (preferably straight sided) and ensure food is cooled before putting in the freezer. Freeze without the lid on, then put on the lid the following day.
6 Check out the Plastic Free July website (plasticfreejuly.org/get-involved/) to find more plastic-free information.

was that they wanted to make changes but weren't always sure how to start.

Perth local Lindsay Miles – now an author and sustainability advocate – signed up for Plastic Free July after seeing a poster in the local library and attending a documentary screening to learn more. Like many, she confessed she didn't think it would be too challenging to avoid plastic. 'When I went home I realised I actually had loads of plastic in my house but I'd never noticed most of it before. I could no longer ignore it.

'In June, I remember going into the supermarket to buy some salad greens. I didn't have a bag, but even though it wasn't yet Plastic Free July I still didn't want to take one. I carried home a handful of loose coriander because I wanted to buy it but I just couldn't take that plastic bag. Now I was aware.'

Lindsay puts the campaign's success down to people being able to identify with simple solutions they could take into their everyday lives and implement right away. It was different to some of the more complex actions to address climate change; for example, calculating carbon offsets could be too technical, and alternatives such as solar panels may have been beyond the reach of many. People could relate to the challenge and make a personal connection.

'They connected, thinking, "Oh, yeah, that's me. I buy carrots and so I too could buy them without a plastic bag." It was about sharing stuff that should have been obvious but it wasn't,' Lindsay says.

'Back in those days there wasn't a lot of information available. There weren't many companies making reusable alternatives. With plastic wrap, for example, it wasn't a matter of going online and ordering a reusable alternative. There was a real need for resourcefulness so we had to talk and share our ideas and solutions.'

Doing it as a collective kept the momentum going and reinforced to all of us that our individual actions were part of something much bigger. There were many stumbling blocks and frustrations in those early days, but in a way that was part of the charm. If it had been effortless, I doubt the creative energy would have flowed and allowed us to grow in the way that we did.

How do we change our buying behaviour?

Our approach to Plastic Free July has always been to start with the basics to ease people into making changes. Making one change is often all the impetus that's needed to start a chain reaction of plastic-free habits. There was a kind of logic in how people tackled this. Often they would start with the basic items, like the Top 4; move on to their shopping needs; start looking at their household decisions in the kitchen, bathroom and laundry; and then make broader life changes. That flow of change became the blueprint for how we organised our resources, and a way to arrange the solutions we shared each week in our newsletters to guide participants. We were working from our own experiences and intuition. Later I learned that much of our approach aligned with theories about behaviour change. I certainly didn't know that in 2013.

If we'd had funding to develop a campaign and tried to own and protect it with strict participation guidelines or restrictions on using our logo, Plastic Free July may not have grown so rapidly or reached so many people. We had nothing more than a hunch and good intentions, but we knew a grassroots approach to reducing plastic was needed and naivety worked in our favour. We were doing and sharing rather than strategising and overthinking; ironically, that ended up growing into a powerful movement for change.

When people joined the Plastic Free July challenge, they had already taken the important first step; it showed that they had started thinking about their plastic use. Rather than suggesting they do a full Earth Carer–style 'bin audit', we encouraged new challenge participants to take a look at the plastics in their bins and in different areas of their lives. This experience was obviously going to be unique for each person, so we urged everyone to start with the 'low-hanging fruit' by choosing one or two plastic items to avoid. Once those new habits started to become second nature, people could move onto the next item. This avoided the temptation for people to bite off more than they could chew, which could lead to them feeling disillusioned and wanting to give up. Small wins inspired further changes, and approaching the challenge this way was more likely to develop long-term habits.

Here's how we approached different aspects of the plastic-free journey and how far we've come since those early days.

Shopping and eating out

A common starting point for people taking on the challenge for the first time was the very visible plastics encountered when out and about. Whether it's grocery shopping, buying a takeaway lunch or dining out, plastics have become integral to the way we store, preserve, transport, buy and consume our food. When we took steps to curb these plastics of convenience, our actions were very visible to others and started some valuable conversations. Beyond simple swaps to avoid the Top 4, the act of trying to avoid single-use plastic also started to change not only how we made our purchases but also what we ate and where we purchased it from.

The idea of a plastic-free 'survival kit' helped people to avoid common encounters with plastic. Our basic kit suggestion included reusable bags, water bottles and coffee cups. By upgrading the kit to include a cloth napkin, plastic-free utensils or an all-in-one bamboo 'spork' (spoon and fork hybrid), and a reusable container, most takeaway packaging or impulse plastic could be avoided, particularly if people put their kit in their bag or an easy-to-access location such as the car or by their front door.

When shopping for groceries, people's first steps often involved switching from items packaged in plastic to those in cardboard packaging or glass that were more readily recycled or reused. Ultimately, though, we knew that just swapping plastic packaging for other materials was creating waste that needed to be managed, so we sought out solutions to avoid packaging altogether – such as purchasing dry goods from bulk sections in health food stores or delicatessens, or taking reusable containers. Again the key was to research availability first and then plan a workable system.

For my own family, I put together a plastic-free shopping kit, with reusable cloth produce bags, a repurposed calico drawstring bag for bread, an assortment of different sized containers, and jars

TAKEAWAY TRIUMPH

Plastic Free July participant Belinda emailed a photo to me of her stainless steel tiffin boxes and insulated bag after we talked about options for buying takeaway.

'Thank you for inspiring me to find a solution for this,' she said. 'I'm very proud of my lovely takeaway "kit" – much more stylish than plastic throwaways, and won't fill me with serious angst any time the family ask for Indian! I've promised to update my friends … it is amazing how interested people are in finding alternatives.'

Belinda first used her kit on a busy night at a Thai restaurant. 'They ended up using seven of my containers and three plastic ones … so I call that a 70% win.'

and bottles for specific refills such as olive oil or washing up liquid. Having it all in one place made the system effortless. When I shared a photo of this kit on social media, it inspired others to put together their own kits.

How far we've come

Plastic-free shopping has become far more achievable in many places since the early years of Plastic Free July. As more and more people have made a commitment to reduce their plastic packaging, the demand for bulk food stores has dramatically increased and supermarkets have started to respond with offerings of bulk nuts or lollies and unpackaged bread. These stores encourage people to bring their own containers for pantry items, personal care and cleaning products, as well as providing reusables and other plastic-free homeware items such as stainless steel pegs and wooden brushes.

Many takeaway outlets offer plastic-free alternatives such as paper or bamboo straws and even discounts for people who bring their own cup. I used to be the only customer to take my own containers to our local Turkish restaurant for our family's takeaway treat of Turkish bread and hummus, which the staff would happily transfer to my containers. They now offer a discount for patrons with BYO containers.

In the kitchen

Prior to doing Plastic Free July, the go-to solution for covering food in our house was inevitably a roll of plastic film. Now we use a variety of alternatives. An easy one is just placing a plate upside down over a bowl of leftovers or putting a cooled-down saucepan straight in the fridge. Most often we store food in reusable containers. The original ones were plastic but over the years we have gradually replaced them with glass or stainless steel. Again, our approach was to first use up what we had before making plastic-free purchases.

I'm not going to pretend it was always an easy transition when we started to avoid plastics. Over the years we attempted to make many items from scratch that typically came in plastic. It could sometimes be time consuming, and relied on us being organised and thinking about what was needed well in advance, as well as being able to withstand the eye-rolls from family members when meal preparation times got a bit out of hand. The first time our family made fresh pasta, it took several hours and resulted in a flour-coated kitchen and hungry kids. Being overly ambitious wasn't a realistic option for busy families trying to do the mad dinner rush, but it was a great weekend activity to enjoy with friends and a chance to make extra for mid-week meals.

For Plastic Free July participants, we tried to offer a range of

> 'As a chef I'm always looking for simple alternatives where I can use bulk supplies to replace plastics. An easy option is to toss pepitas in soy sauce and bake in the oven for a delicious salad topping. A great plastic-free snack is to buy bulk nuts and warm on the stovetop with olive oil, and add sprigs of rosemary.'
>
> – Virginia, Plastic Free July participant

options so people could choose what best suited them depending on availability, budget and time. Dips and crackers are a good example of how simple or complicated solutions could be. Guacamole could be made in just a couple of minutes with an avocado, lemon, oil, salt and pepper, whereas hummus took more time, requiring chickpeas to be soaked overnight and then cooked. Crackers were hard to find without any plastic packaging but could be substituted with carrot and celery sticks or made by thinly slicing a baguette, brushing the slices with olive oil and baking them in the oven until golden brown. For those with more time, we had recipes to make your own crackers.

Over time, newfound alternatives became habits. I often cook extra chickpeas and kidney beans to freeze in glass jars for future meals and keep 'emergency items' such as extra coffee beans or a knob of fresh ginger for grating in the freezer.

Yes, preparing meals in this way can be more time consuming, but many people found other benefits in being organised and planning meals. Buying just what was needed reduced food waste (and therefore cost). Avoiding plastic packaging also tended to result in a healthier diet as it cut out highly processed foods and those that contained preservatives or environmentally unsustainable ingredients such as palm oil. Taking time was not always such a bad thing. I remember one night my son Leeuwin wanted garlic bread as part of a birthday dinner; the ten minutes we spent chopping garlic and parsley, mixing in butter and spreading it between slices of a baguette were also spent chatting about his day. It was the most I had heard him talk in weeks. There is no denying the benefits of convenience foods packaged in plastic, but there are costs involved that go beyond waste.

How far we've come

The top drawer in my kitchen where I kept plastic cling film now holds a variety of reusable containers, insulated flasks, tiffin pans and wraps – they are among the items we use the most. In the bottom drawer lies an unfinished roll of cling film from 2011 – we joke that it will be our children's inheritance.

Beeswax wraps are now readily available to purchase, and many schools and community groups hold make-your-own days. Reusable produce bags make it possible to purchase fruit and vegetables without plastic packaging.

Cleaning our bodies and homes

Bathrooms and laundries were the next areas people turned to when reducing household plastic. Some items could be avoided by relatively simple swaps such as switching from liquid soap to bar soap – after all, it wasn't that long ago that bar soap was the only choice. Even this created lively discussions on social media, which showed how much we'd become conditioned to plastic dispensers. One parent of young children posted, 'Can young children be taught to wash their hands properly using bar soap?' My answer to this was a resounding yes, though I admitted it could get a little messy.

Other alternatives included toilet rolls wrapped in paper, bamboo toothbrushes, laundry powder in cardboard boxes, and refilling bottles with laundry liquids and other cleaning products. Vinegar and bicarb (baking) soda became our household cleaning mainstays, along with other natural products such as lemons, eucalyptus oil and soapnuts.

Not all options were available in bulk, completely plastic free or affordable to all participants, but there was no shortage of ideas as people shared their cleaning tips and DIY recipes.

Different solutions worked for different people – I started using solid shampoo bars to wash my hair whereas some of our group chose the bicarb and apple cider vinegar method referred to as 'no poo'. Others refilled their existing containers with shampoo and conditioner from bulk suppliers.

We always encouraged people to use what they had while it remained functional. Participant Lindsay Miles said it took her around 18 months to use up all the plastic items in her bathroom.

For girls and women, reusable menstrual products such as cloth pads, menstrual cups and specially designed underwear are all good options to avoid plastics found in disposable menstrual products and their packaging. While making the switch to reusables to reduce waste I've also discovered there can be significant long-term cost savings and research shows these alternatives can be effective. A scientific review of menstrual cups published in the journal *Lancet Public Health* in 2019 indicates they are safe and result in similar or lower amounts of leakage than disposable pads or tampons. The study also found they are still a little-known option worldwide, which is concerning given that not having effective ways of managing menstruation can affect girls' schooling and women's experience of work all over the world. The benefits of reusables can go beyond avoiding waste.

I'd like to see a lot more awareness and education for girls and women on reusable options for what the scientists refer to as 'menstruation management'. Menstrual cups are not a new invention but, once again, marketing has sold us the convenience of disposable solutions without considering the environmental impact of up to 11 000 single-use menstrual products per person entering landfill over that one person's lifetime.

How far we've come

Pre-used shampoo bottles can now be refilled from bulk stores. Keeping these items in the home stops them from going into landfill. Shampoo bars, once the domain of specialty stores, are now appearing in major supermarkets as well as being readily available at markets, online, and in bulk or health food stores. Sustainably grown and biodegradable bamboo toothbrushes are a staple in many bathrooms and recycled, paper-wrapped toilet paper is now available in bulk.

Broader life changes

As we progressed, we became far more alert to our reliance on plastic – it really was everywhere. We shared ideas that came directly from the Plastic Free July group; these were tried-and-true solutions.

At Christmas and for celebrations we suggested homemade gifts and shared the Japanese art of furoshiki – wrapping gifts in fabric. We also encouraged vouchers for experiences or our time. Buying stationery and school supplies was often tricky, with even a couple of pens or pencils packaged in plastic – again the solution was often to go to smaller stores. My personal favourite swap was finding a thick wooden pencil with a fluorescent lead to replace a plastic highlighter pen that ran out – it's still going strong today and will probably never need replacing.

There were always lots of questions about pets, such as the inevitable 'How do I pick up dog poo without a plastic bag?' Our solutions ranged from a DIY 'dog poo worm farm' under an ornamental tree, to picking up dog poo with the wrappings from toilet paper. The ideas were as diverse as the people participating and to this day are a work in progress.

With July being the start of the summer break in the northern hemisphere (and shorter winter school holidays in the south), many participants spent a good part of Plastic Free July travelling and on holidays. Being away from home meant avoiding plastic could be even more challenging than usual, but by packing lightweight reusable bags, water bottles, cups and utensils, travel solutions were more achievable. We even encouraged people to pack their own earphones, and warm wraps or scarves, to reduce airline packaging.

Sometimes it felt that for every plastic item we tried to avoid, another would appear in its place. Trying to grow herbs and vegetables was daunting when faced with seedlings in plastic punnets and compost in plastic bags. We just had to remember our mantra of using what we had, sharing solutions, buying secondhand and supporting local independent stores – these changes together went a long way towards reducing our reliance on plastic.

How far we've come

Giving experiences as gifts means less waste and an opportunity to spend time with people we care about. Some of our favourite vouchers include breakfast at a café, a cup of tea in bed, a lemon foot bath and theatre tickets. It's an idea that has been taken up more widely now; in 2019 Berlin's rubbish collection service even launched an advertising campaign urging the city's residents to cut down on waste by gifting time and experiences rather than material objects.

Airline headphones are often no longer in plastic bags. Some airlines have replaced multiple plastic containers on meal trays with cardboard trays and boxes.

Nurseries are starting to offer plant pots made from natural materials such as paper pulp and coir, and some act as a collection point for plastic items.

Sharing the inspiration

In 2013, we really started to see an increase in people taking Plastic Free July beyond making changes in their own lives and sharing what they were doing in a variety of creative ways. People reported feeling really positive about what they had managed to achieve and they wanted to pass this on to others, which kept the momentum going. Something I have always really appreciated is how incredibly generous our community has been about spreading the message and sharing their stories of change. Their insights were gifts to everyone participating and their enthusiasm encouraged others to join in.

For some, that sharing started with friends and family and then extended into the community. People would often come to the challenge after first observing someone already doing it.

Even though we encouraged people to start small, a few people did go 'cold turkey' and tried to avoid all plastics. Some, like young New Zealand couple Jessie Fitzgerald and Nathan Rushton, went even further, making it their New Year's resolution to do the challenge for a whole year after their first Plastic Free July. They had so much knowledge and were happy to share their ideas, speak at our events and answer lots of tricky questions people had about avoiding plastics.

One of the challenge's original participants, Jane Genovese, is an educator who created colourful mindmaps to help people understand different topics. In 2013 during Plastic Free July she created a mindmap called 'Plastic Detox: Deplastify Your Life', with simple eye-catching graphics that helped people visualise the different ways they could harness their plastic-free potential. As soon as I

FAMILY CHALLENGE

Lucie Labrecque and family

Participants, Plastic Free July

Lucie Labrecque confessed that she originally thought it was 'really weird' to even be focusing on the amount of rubbish we were producing. 'It was totally off my radar,' she says. At the time Lucie was starting to become aware of the importance of making better choices but it was only after hearing about the facilities where our waste went that she described a 'feeling that something had shifted'.

Starting out

Lucie, her husband Russell and their children discussed Plastic Free July and what they could do. They began with the Top 4 because, Lucie says, 'We didn't know how else we could do it'. That approach was one that Plastic Free July has always encouraged. It was all about keeping it achievable and celebrating the little victories, which carried the momentum through.

'I tried to focus on the things I knew I could succeed with and went from there,' Lucie remembers. She took a reusable kit with her when she was out and about; it contained a cup, reusable bags and containers. Lucie then went on to source bulk items and started going to farmers' markets each week.

Solutions at school

Lucie and Russell's daughter Sacha was 12 when the family started Plastic Free July. She remembers how it spread from her mum initiating household changes to other family members joining in.

'It was always Mum at the start. Dad has slowly got on board in the last few years. He still struggles with it not being as convenient, but he's now making the changes himself. For me it became natural so quickly that now I don't really remember the time before.'

When Sacha started high school, the changes at home were in stark contrast to the amount of plastic packaging she noticed in her school canteen. 'I saw there was nothing being done at school, not even recycling, and I thought, "It's so normal for me – why isn't it normal for all these people when they have the time and resources and energy to make it normal?"'

Everything sold at the school canteen was wrapped in plastic. As environment captain, Sacha initiated conversations with the canteen managers and this led to really valuable changes such as removing straws, switching to bamboo cutlery and paper plates, and offering self-serve options to replace individually wrapped items.

Waste at work

Lucie and Russell's son Kieran, a diesel mechanic, now goes to the farmers' market with his girlfriend Paris most weeks, and they take their own bags and breakfast dishes.

When his mum started going plastic free it was an 'abrupt change', Kieran recalls, but then it soon became the new normal.

In terms of Kieran's work environment, he says that 'industry still has a long way to go', with no incentive for changes to the way that mechanical parts arrive wrapped in plastic. New workplace habits are forming, though, with water dispensers in the workshops, though Kieran is the only one who takes a reusable cup. 'People don't even stop and think that these things are going to last for millions of years,' he says.

Paris has noticed others nurses at the hospital where she works catching onto using reusable cups after seeing hers. 'It keeps the coffee warmer for longer when we finally get a chance to drink it,' she says.

Practical results

The results of these practical lifestyle changes have been impressive. Lucie's family found they saved a lot of money, halved their recycling and reduced their general waste so much that they no longer need to put out their landfill bin every week.

'Although we are not totally plastic free, we have been able to significantly reduce the plastic we have in our lives,' says Lucie.

posted this on our Facebook page it received incredibly positive feedback. It has since been shared thousands of times around the world and translated into Croatian and Spanish. As always, the creativity and ideas came from personal experience.

On the mindmap Jane gave tips for food preparation such as learning to cook from scratch. One of her ventures involved a ravioli-making session with friends. 'Not only did we produce a delicious meal but we had a wonderful afternoon together full of laughter and fun,' she wrote. (You can find the original mindmap, and Jane's thoughts on going plastic free, at learningfundamentals.com.au.)

From participants to change makers

Some people started branching out in their Plastic Free July challenge by giving talks, writing articles, starting blogs and eventually even writing books; this diversified the information that was available, responding to those on independent paths and at different stages of their plastic-free journey. The plastic-free and zero-waste movement has grown and there is now so much information thanks to a growing number of mentors championing the message.

Blogs including Lindsay Miles' *Treading My Own Path* and Erin Rhoads' *The Rogue Ginger* are written by early participants of Plastic Free July; both writers have since published books on reducing our waste. Lindsay Miles started the *Treading My Own Path* blog in 2013 and when I chatted to her, we agreed that one of the key ways the momentum kept going was people engaging in discussions and asking lots of questions.

The comments from participants were often more important than what we wrote and shared. These were people who were all living the challenge in different ways, and their experiences really helped us to keep growing and learning. Many of the solutions involved going back to how we used to live without plastic, rather than finding new and innovative solutions. We benefited from looking back to what people did in a time where disposables weren't the go-to response. 'There is just so much knowledge in the world,' Lindsay points out. 'We weren't trying to reinvent the wheel; we were really just remembering how to make the wheel.'

For other participants, the challenge of doing Plastic Free July became a springboard for new business ventures. After doing the challenge, Perth residents Amanda Welschbillig and Jeannie Richardson found tracking down plastic-free products was unsustainable. They had to travel more than 45 minutes and go to several shops to source unpackaged products, so they were substituting one problem with another through food miles and extra time. Necessity

> 'When we didn't have plastic film, we used greaseproof paper for wrapping a sandwich and if there were leftovers we generally put them in the fridge uncovered or sometimes used a plate as a cover. We also used brown paper for a lot of things; I remember my mum used to line cake tins with the paper that had wrapped the butter.'
>
> – Vicki, Plastic Free July participant

led to innovation and, in 2015, the friends opened their own shop called Wasteless Pantry, stocking bulk groceries, pantry and laundry items, and, wherever possible, supporting local producers to reduce food miles and also refill bulk food containers to reduce 'behind-the-scenes' packaging. It was a leap of faith, but like many of us, they'd had an informal apprenticeship in retail and knew what was needed.

'We both did all the shopping for our families, so we did have some experience,' Jeannie says.

At Wasteless Pantry, Amanda and Jeannie's priorities are reducing packaging and food miles. Customers bring their own containers to be filled and measuring cups help people to only purchase what they need. Community spirit is strengthened through a space for locals to share their excess garden produce for free; Amanda and Jeannie give regular talks, and encourage the community and businesses in their area to join the Plastic Free July challenge.

'Wasteless Pantry walks a fine and sometimes difficult line between activism and commercially viable enterprise,' Jeannie says. The duo stand by their 'buy what you need' motto, which challenges the current retail message to customers to 'buy more, spend more, consume more', and they apply this across all aspects of their business. One of their stores produces a mere 1.7 kilograms of waste a month (roughly 2 per cent of the amount generated by the average household) while selling unpackaged food to feed hundreds of households.

'We seem to be at the tipping point of public understanding that our actions have an impact for better or worse,' Amanda observes. 'Plastic Free July gives practical solutions to what can seem to be overwhelming change that is needed, offering a community approach where individual action all adds up.'

'It's our "Ground Zero,"' Jeannie adds. She describes the annual challenge as 'our time to reflect and reaffirm our core values – why we started down this path in the first place'.

New habits, new questions

At the end of each July it was time to take stock and review the changes we had made. We had formed new habits but found that others changes were difficult to continue, and there were always new challenges that we vowed to try 'next July'. As always, there were compromises, especially when choices affect others and there are considerations beyond plastic.

My colleague Amy's son wasn't so keen on homemade toothpaste. My children loved burritos filled with refried beans and salad but didn't like the corn tortillas we made with masa. I couldn't find anywhere to buy them plastic free and since it was a healthy meal that everyone in the family enjoyed we still buy the packaged version. At the end of the day it's important to focus on what we can avoid.

•

By concentrating on plastics it was difficult at times to respond to concerns about other environmental issues. Sharing photos of taking containers to the butcher resulted in complaints of 'If you really cared about the planet you wouldn't eat meat', and taking reusables on an aeroplane received comments about the carbon footprint of air travel. Of course plastic pollution is only one of many environmental issues but it does have flow-on effects. Avoiding plastic meant people couldn't buy meat from a supermarket and had to go to the butcher, which often reduced their consumption of meat to maybe once a week, and many people reported moving to a more plant-based diet. For others, reducing their plastic footprint was the first step to reducing their carbon footprint.

The most important thing is that we were doing it with a support network that struggled with the same problems – and found ways to overcome them. Making changes and sharing stories was starting to spread. It led to new expectations within ourselves, and lasting habits for our families and for the growing Plastic Free July community.

7
It's all about the sharing

A week before the challenge, one year I ducked into the Emu Point Cafe in Albany, Western Australia, to grab a coffee on my way to addressing the local community. People were sipping coffee and looking out at the tranquil harbour. Against that backdrop, a blackboard message above a basket of cups caught my eye:

> Recycled mugs to take away. Reduce use of paper cups!
> If possible please return. Drop off unwanted mugs here!

Coffee in hand, I sat by the waterfront where the waters of Oyster Harbour flow through a narrow channel. Nestled between houses and the café on one side and coastal bushland on the other, the water travels into Frenchman Bay and ultimately the Southern Ocean. It is a mesmerising place that always reminds me of our close connection to the ocean.

Despite the serene outlook, my 'to do' list kept niggling away at me. It had been a couple of days since I'd written a social media post, and I didn't have anything prepared. Our posts for Plastic Free July continued to be spontaneous – we shared photos of our efforts or the initiatives we came across to reduce plastic waste as we went about our day-to-day lives. It was a far cry from an Insta-perfect communications strategy. I would call it organic – or, as my less diplomatic Gen Z daughter Pepita puts it, 'out of focus'.

I asked the barista about the sign on the basket of cups. She told me that most cups were donated by the community and that they were available for people to borrow for their takeaway coffee if they hadn't brought a reusable one. It seemed like a simple yet effective idea that I thought would grab other people's attention. Social media post problem solved! I posted a photo with the caption:

> @emupointcafe has a basket of reusable cups for people to use for takeaway coffee and then return next time. Great to see business taking practical steps to be part of the solution!

I didn't dwell on it too much, so I was pretty amazed to wake the next day to news that the basket-of-cups photo had gone viral overnight, with thousands of people around the world engaging with and sharing it.

Returning to the café, I chatted to the barista about the photo's success and ended up in the kitchen with owner Kate Marwick, who seemed as surprised as I was. Sure, it was a wonderful idea, but why would a basket of cups have such a massive impact? The answer was quite enchanting. Melissa Joan Hart had shared it. I had to admit that I didn't know who she was. Kate told me she was the star of the 1990s TV show *Sabrina the Teenage Witch*. Kate had grown up watching the show, so she was thrilled by the Instagram repost and Melissa's great message:

> I LOVE this idea to reduce single-use plastic waste!! Let's #stopsucking … on straws and make a move away from plastics that aren't reusable this #PlasticFreeJuly. Start with the straw in

July and see if you can start new habits that will stick. Follow @plasticfreejuly to get some ideas.

In her hometown of Westport, Connecticut, Melissa was on her own mission to get her town to go plastic straw-free by promising to share social media posts of restaurants that agreed to only provide paper straws on request.

After Plastic Free July's photo went viral, the Emu Point Cafe story reached national media. Kate was blown away by the flow-on effects of one photo and it remains one of Plastic Free July's most popular and commented on social media posts.

I often reflect on why it has been so powerful. I put it down to the simplicity of the idea. Café owner Kate agrees, saying it's about just using what we have. I think everyone can identify with the photo and see themselves being able to do it. We all have cups that we could take to a café and most of us probably have a few extra that we could donate. It's not such a stretch of the imagination to think, yes, I could confidently suggest this to my local café and it would not take a lot for their staff to implement. It's eye-catching too: a basket of colourful mismatched mugs and a friendly handwritten sign on a chalkboard. That's not hard for any business to contemplate.

Sharing the photo on social media resulted in hundreds of people tagging their local cafés and suggesting they replicate the idea. It was really exciting to see cafés around the world saying they would give the initiative a go. Others offered to donate cups to their favourite café, so it garnered significant support from customers and local businesses.

For Emu Point Cafe, the basket of cups was a natural progression.

'It's quite a community-based café and people literally live just next door, so many already brought their own cups,' Kate says. 'It came from the idea of taking things back to basics. It was just about trying to reduce waste by using what we already have.'

> 'As a society, we seem to rush around a lot these days. We've been using cups for centuries. I don't really know why but all of a sudden we started using these cups with lids and had to be on the go at all times.'
>
> – Kate Marwick, owner, Emu Point Cafe

There was a strong local sentiment about reducing waste, and Kate's initiative was another example of that getting-back-to-basics community vibe that seems to take hold when people search for ways to move away from mass production and consumption. The cups don't always return, but donations more than make up for any cups that happen to find a new home.

'I don't see why there's a need to put deposits down on reusables. I think if there is trust, people normally do the right thing. We get lots coming back but lots of new ones as well,' Kate says.

Emu Point is a place where treading lightly extends from the coastline's sweep of sand to business awareness. The environmental benefits and customer support have overwhelmingly outweighed any early-day inconveniences. 'Café owners get quite scared about anything new and different that might slow them down. It can be a little tricky, but that's our job,' says Kate. 'Our job is to make coffee and it doesn't really matter what vessel it's in.'

How people share the challenge

The basket of cups at Emu Point Cafe showed the power of individual change. People identified with the initiative, saw how simple it was, and wanted to share the portable, positive idea with their communities. Again, the impact came from lots of ordinary people getting on board to make small changes.

People loved participating in Plastic Free July because it gave them an opportunity to act on a problem that concerned them instead of feeling disempowered or unsure about what steps to take. Of course there were challenges, but it was balanced by feedback from people who told us that they felt healthier, happier and more connected with their communities, as well as feeling good about an emptier bin or less plastic in their pantries or bathrooms. These changes were infectious – when people feel positive about making a difference, it is natural to want to share that with others. The question was how to do this and where to start – and the answer could be as simple as a basket of cups and a blackboard sign.

Our Plastic Free July participants were all ages and came from all walks of life; there wasn't a certain 'type'. For many, doing the challenge was their first step towards trying to live more sustainably. They didn't consider themselves environmental activists and they wanted to share ideas and solutions in a way that wasn't seen to be criticising other people's behaviour or nagging them to 'do the right thing'. The flow-on effect of reducing individual plastic use is seeing it everywhere, but also noticing the extent of other people's disposable lifestyles. How was it possible to navigate this without being viewed as a nagger or a self-righteous pain in the neck? The 'How could you use that straw; haven't you heard about the one in the turtle's nose?' dialogue may have been tempting, but it ran the risk of disengaging or embarrassing others. That was the last thing we wanted. They were difficult conversations to have, especially during those years when the problem wasn't yet on people's radar.

So the next obvious step for Plastic Free July was helping people to share their experiences of the challenge, because seeing what others did was often all the impetus that others needed. Again, we didn't know how to do this, but we had been trying different strategies ourselves. We were in the wonderfully privileged position of being supported by a growing number of people who were in it for the right reasons, who weren't politicising the issue or alienating others. The tools and resources we came up with were all 'open source', which meant they were taken up and spread quickly. Plastic Free July wasn't just designed for everyday people; it was also *created* by them. We took the journey together.

In 2013, our third year of the challenge, Gabrielle Grime joined the Earth Carers waste education team. For Gabrielle, one of the best things about those early days was seeing personal change spread to others.

'It's been one of the greatest experiences of my life. The fact that it struck a chord with so many people was really fantastic,' she says. 'Every day there would be another story. That it is still continuing and people have it as part of their lives now is pretty amazing.'

Our salaries were covered but there was no budget to design programs so that brought its own challenges, but also a level of freedom since we weren't restricted by guidelines or protocols. 'When we realised what was successful, it was just a matter of: "What else can we do to add to the success?" That was probably fairly unique, even for local government,' Gabrielle remembers. 'So we had the ability to think laterally, try different things and off we went.'

The plastic-free morning tea

Bringing people together around food seemed like a good way to start having conversations. It would also be a tangible and delicious way to showcase plastic-free ideas. Gabrielle described it as being a gentle way to introduce it to colleagues and friends: 'friendly and not too full on'. Instead of criticising or saying, 'Don't do that', a morning tea was an invitation to join in by showing how it could be done: 'Here, you can do this'.

The first step in creating the initiative was to hold a morning tea for the rest of our staff. We took cloth bags to the local bakery, bought fruit bread and used our trusty office teapot (our tea and coffee were already purchased in bulk). Gabrielle baked muffins and cake, and prepared dips served with vegetable sticks and a fruit platter.

Before we enjoyed our plastic-free feast, I photographed it to use in the simple package we'd put together on our website. People could organise catering for the morning tea or invite everyone to bring a share plate (both of these could be mini challenges in themselves). We figured it could be done among friends, in workplaces, at schools or in community groups. The initiative was simply a guide with ideas to help people get started. Resources included steps to organise a morning tea, template invitations incorporating our photos, a plastic pollution quiz and recipes. To get the message across, we chronicled our own morning tea through photos, the 'No Plastic Please' sign we gave caterers, and our experiences of navigating any tricky questions from staff or suppliers.

After every event or talk, we invited people to choose one thing they could do about the plastics problem. It could be as simple as telling someone about what they had learned, vowing to remember a reusable coffee cup or looking for plastic-free alternatives in local stores. Our 'Plastic Free Pledge' template also helped people to be more accountable. Like setting a goal, writing a pledge played a motivating role and reinforced group challenges such as the morning tea.

Pretty much instantaneously the idea of the plastic-free morning tea took off. It really struck a chord. People started sharing photos – from multinational tech company Adobe brainstorming plastic-free ideas on the windows of their offices overlooking Sydney's skyline, to a couple hiking in Alaska who shared a photo of their morning tea picnic in the forest.

At the Western Australian Marine Science Institution, Angela Rossen thought having a morning tea would be a great way to share the challenge with scientists and colleagues. 'Having the morning tea was an excuse to come together and do something that was fun, and

MORNING TEA TIPS

- Hold your 'plastic-free' morning tea in the lead-up to Plastic Free July or during July, so it is part of a global event.
- Do research and speak with local stores well in advance of the event. We found a local bakery that was happy to use our containers if we dropped them off beforehand.
- Make it fun and inviting for people to participate rather than it being onerous or 'educational'.

the whole team was invited to contribute to the event,' she says. 'It wasn't about proselytising but the opportunity to come together to do something positive.'

To her surprise, some of the plastic pollution quiz statistics shocked even her colleagues and started discussions on ways to reduce plastic use. 'One of the good things about having the morning tea was because we work in the same space, the conversations continued, and we could see what the others were doing … and what people were putting in their bins. It helped to keep us on track.'

People on a mission

Some people dedicated their single-use plastic mission to a particular cause. Earth Carers volunteer Columba Tierney's approach was one that couldn't be ignored. In 2013, armed with signs saying 'The Last Straw', she mobilised a Straw Army with herself as Honorary Sergeant Major Straw and marched the streets of Perth with her troops, encouraging businesses to hide their straws behind the counter and to offer them only on request.

'Striving for plastic free and zero waste living is a way of protesting against a wasteful society and saying we can do better.'

– Tammy Logan, blogger and speaker, *Gippsland Unwrapped*

Columba had so much energy and passion. Her army uniform was probably a startling motivator too. We printed signs and shared photos of the Straw Army posing with local businesses. Back then the problem of plastic straws was only just beginning to emerge but it wasn't long before enquiries started coming in as people realised this was a single item they could tackle. We added these resources to the growing toolkit of ideas on the website.

Tammy Logan from rural Victoria first took part in Plastic Free July in 2015 and kept going. Now an advocate of waste-free living and public speaker, Tammy writes a blog called *Gippsland Unwrapped.*

She describes completing the challenge as 'one of the most positive things I've ever done'. 'It revealed to me that I have choices and I do have power to effect change. I didn't start this lifestyle because I had lots of spare time; I made specific decisions about how I wanted to lead my life and guide my family to better reflect my values.'

People like Tammy shine a light on consumption and help others find ways to do better. When some participants found their cups and reusables were being refused due to 'health and safety regulations', Tammy's research unearthed the facts. The Australia New Zealand Food Standards Code doesn't contain any legislative requirements that prevent a business from using a customer's BYO containers. Sharing her well-researched blog post equipped many of our participants to understand the issue and navigate any situations where their plastic-free choices were questioned.

Waste-wise communities

Plastic-free initiatives spread into local communities through simple ideas that caught on and multiplied. Sometimes it happened through existing groups but in many cases people came together to form new ones. These groups have championed the vibrant grassroots movement that Plastic Free July has become, and over the years it's been a privilege to speak at their events. From movie nights to plastic-free picnics and 'long table lunches', workshops, beach clean-ups and festivals, there is no end to the creative ways communities participate in the challenge. It's where I learn about the issues and challenges and, most importantly, the stories of change that inspire others.

For many communities, participating in Plastic Free July has become something of an annual ritual, with each new year building on ideas, tackling another plastic item and getting more people involved.

Cape to Cape Plastic Free, Western Australia

In 2013 the Cape to Cape Plastic Free group in Margaret River, Western Australia, was the first group we came across outside Perth to run Plastic Free July as a community-wide initiative. They are still going. As convenor Laura Bailey says, 'When you have your eyes open to it you can't unsee it … people could just see single-use plastics everywhere. Everyone showed an interest and wanted to be part of it.'

Each year has unearthed more issues that the group addresses through working with cafés, retail stores and supermarkets. As they spread the challenge, more local cafés joined the Responsible Cafes program, offering customers a discount for bringing reusable cups and starting conversations around plastic reduction. The group also ran a popular monthly wash-up station and provided cups for the coffee vans at their farmers' market, which led to a government grant to set up a mobile Wash Against Waste trailer to house their equipment and allow them to offer the service to other events in the region.

Cape to Cape Plastic Free also started making reusable 'Boomerang Bags' as a way of kickstarting their town to stop using plastic shopping bags. Along with local schools, they held sewing bees and made hundreds of bags with donated fabric. The bags were then distributed to busy shopping areas in the town.

'If people forgot their own bags, they could easily grab one,' Laura Bailey explains. 'It's an honesty system, like a library book. It's giving people real ownership.'

Mullum Cares, New South Wales

Mullumbimby in the Byron Shire of northern New South Wales has been transformed through the Mullum Cares group that helped many town traders kick the plastic bag habit through Plastic Free July and beyond. The local IGA dropped their supply of 150 000 plastic bags a year after locals enthusiastically supported a plastic bag-free trial. A crowdfunded filtered-water fountain was also launched to coincide with the Mullum Music Festival, an event that stopped using plastic cups and bottles. Businesses have swapped balloons for eco-friendly fabric bunting.

Home Environmental Network, Western Australia

In the coastal town of Esperance, Western Australia, Sue Starr and volunteers from the Home Environmental Network shared Plastic Free July by setting themselves up at the local supermarket where they made and gave away reusable produce bags from secondhand net curtains.

A TOWN GETS INVOLVED

Merren Tait and the town of Raglan

Plastic-free initiatives, Raglan, New Zealand

In the small coastal town of Raglan, on New Zealand's North Island, librarian Merren Tait went online to look for solutions after seeing images of albatrosses feeding plastic to their young. 'It needed to be something everyone could do, something my community could do,' she said.

Merren came across the Plastic Free July challenge and, not one to do things by halves, decided to participate for a whole year in 2013 – and got the town involved too. Not only did Merren do the challenge for a whole year, but she didn't buy any plastic at all. Single-use or otherwise. At the time, it was the first overseas Plastic Free July initiative we had come across.

All Raglan's cafés participated and offered discounts for reusable cups. Their chalkboard signs offered rallying slogans such as, 'We're supporting Plastic Free July: no to single-use drink bottles and straws. Give it a go!'

Local grocery stores had a reusable bag bank and the town pub put their plastic straws away. Participants gathered at the pub on Friday nights for a Plastics Anonymous support group to share their dilemmas and ideas. Even the town's adventure cycling race, the Karioi Classic, got involved by offering water refill stations rather than disposable cups, and making cable ties for bike number plates made out of leaves from native cabbage trees.

> These initiatives are all run by different groups and the momentum has continued. 'Plastic is obvious,' Merren says. 'People can see it and its effects and the immediacy of the problem. It is something people can do something about pretty easily and feel good by just making one little change.'

Plastic Free Launceston, Tasmania

Trish Haeusler from Launceston, Tasmania, can't remember how she first heard of Plastic Free July, but she knew it was important. 'A bloke once told me of a concept of having an "encore" when you get older ... using your skills and experience and relating them to something that's important to you. I thought, yep, this is my encore. I'm going to use the skills that I've got to actually do something.'

Trish started up a Plastic Free Launceston Facebook page to see if there were others who felt the same. It was slow going to begin with, but then it took off. The group spread the message by sharing the Plastic Free July challenge on social media, visiting schools, giving talks, encouraging businesses, and attending local community events and markets with solution-focused displays.

'Plastic Free July needs to be seen as the greatest hook on which we've attached ourselves. It would have been, I think, much more difficult for us to do what we're doing without it,' Trish says.

Local government leaders

Local governments, councils and municipalities are usually the agencies that deal with litter and waste management. With their responsibility for delivering services and managing amenities, they are also closely connected to communities. The Earth Carers program I worked for during Plastic Free July's inception was based in local government, and many other councils were early adopters of the challenge. Councils have since championed the challenge in inventive ways.

For councils in our region, involvement would often start with a staff morning tea but then roll out to other areas across their operations and into the community. The City of Subiaco in Perth's inner west did a coffee cup challenge and gave reusable coffee cups to staff who had signed up for Plastic Free July. During the month, staff would take it in turns to get coffee from different cafés; these 'blind tastings' led to a voting process to nominate the overall favourite café in the suburbs.

Reducing plastic at local events

Local government staff started to work with event organisers to initiate plastic reduction ideas. Over a couple of years we helped the Town of Claremont, 8 kilometres south-west of the Perth CBD, to work with coffee and food vendors at their annual Celebrate Lake Claremont event. One of the first steps was to develop an application process for vendors to ensure they would not use any plastic packaging for food serviceware. No single-use plastic items were permitted to be given away or sold, and craft activities such as woodworking with recycled timber were provided.

Instead of the secondhand mugs that we used at our own events, we purchased a set of 100 lime-green coffee cups that could stack together into tubs. At the event, our volunteers delivered these to the coffee van, which made taking orders and serving coffee at a busy event easy. We then placed labelled containers in convenient locations and set up a wash-up station with our Earth Carers volunteers

KITTING OUT AN EVENT

Our event kit contained 100 coffee cups, a set of clear acrylic stackable cups that could be used for smoothies, and long-handled metal teaspoons. These were stored in tubs, which could then be used for the washing up and to collect the cups and drop them back to the coffee vans. We included washing up equipment: an urn to heat water, dishwashing liquid, sanitising liquid, scrubbing brush and tea towels. We also included washing station signage and a 'how-to' guide with instructions for washing up to meet council health guidelines.

that used sufficient hot water and rinsing to meet the council's health guidelines. Portable water refill stations with built-in filters that attached to outdoor taps, and a set of reusable water cups, meant sales of bottled water could be banned. Doing the research and organising a full event kit enabled the resources to be available for other groups. The event kit significantly reduced waste disposal costs for the Celebrate Lake Claremont event, and litter became non-existent.

Council initiatives

Clean-ups in local parks, on beaches and along waterways were popular events for local governments to run during Plastic Free July. These also provide insights into commonly littered items that councils can address through policies and regulations. Librarians created displays and ran workshops, talks and school holiday craft activities for children introducing ways to reduce plastic in fun and engaging ways.

Over the last ten years I've watched as an increasing number of local authorities introduce measures to reduce waste at events and implement bans on problem litter items, such as banning smoking on beaches and helium-balloon releases. Local-level initiatives often pave the way for state- and national-level change.

Bega Valley Shire Council in south-east New South Wales used Plastic Free July resources to inspire a number of community initiatives, and to motivate their staff to make changes. 'Our library at Tura Beach implemented a mug library and we shared ideas for reducing plastic waste,' waste project officer Sarah Eastman says.

The council stocked up on bags for the main office's Boomerang Bag station, and also spread the message to 8500 people through a competition, with prize bags containing books, food wraps, and reusable coffee cups and water bottles. A free beeswax wrap workshop gave council members a chance to bond with people 'passionate about reducing waste'. It was a two-way street: council staff were able to share their expertise, but were also inspired 'by some fantastic thoughts and ideas from the community', Sarah says.

Prompting a change from within

Plastic Free July doesn't just make changes at a community and council level; it also helps to bring staff together. Rebecca Brown, manager of waste and recycling at the WA Local Government Association, says Plastic Free July events and morning teas are a regular calendar fixture in their office. 'It's great to see how it engages different people across [our] organisation to change their behaviour, initially for a month but then long term as well.'

Competitions to reduce plastic use have helped to increase staff

> 'Plastic Free July is a great initiative ... a simple idea that draws attention to a big problem, then hooks into and captures the public's imagination.'
>
> – Geoff Atkinson, communication and education manager, Mindarie Regional Council

morale through the ideas that are shared; they involve all members of the organisation, not just those from the environment and waste team. 'This year our superstar winner was a member of the industrial relations team, who picked up litter, reduced his own single-use plastic and engaged his family in the challenge,' Rebecca says.

'Our involvement in Plastic Free July made me realise just how many people in the organisation are actively engaged in reducing their waste. It makes me feel immensely proud to be part of an organisation with such wonderful and caring people. I also love reminding everyone that Plastic Free July was a local government *and* a Western Australian initiative that has gone global.'

Schools and universities

Many young people want to act on plastic pollution and drive change; millennials and Gen Z-ers show great concern about environmental issues. Plastic Free July has been adopted by preschools and childcare centres, schools, colleges, universities and other educational institutions, initiated by students, parents, teachers and administrators alike. Addressing plastic pollution can and does form part of the curriculum. I've seen it delivered as part of science and mathematics, creative arts and language lessons; in sustainability efforts; through community services; and in whole-of-school events.

As the month of July coincides with summer or winter holidays in most parts of the world, some schools participate at other times of the year, or plan a day or week of activities. Again, by being flexible, the challenge has spread deeply and widely. A strong part of Plastic Free July's attraction is that it offers students something proactive and tangible to do, rather than just leaving them to feel overwhelmed by despair.

Environmental awareness has definitely grown among students.

I'm always struck by their understanding and knowledge of our impacts on the world, and compare this to my own education when issues of pollution and climate change weren't taught at all. Education can also be a two-way street. I was recently involved in research for a ban on plastic bags in my state and heard a number of older people saying they'd heard about the plastic pollution problem from their grandchildren.

At Margaret River Primary School in Western Australia, teacher Liz Angell has described Plastic Free July as 'a real winner', with huge support from the canteen staff and students as well as the parents.

'One of the most effective things I found was that once we started, we found so many more options where we could recycle our plastic waste,' Liz says. The canteen switched from plastic cutlery to bamboo, plastic straws to paper straws, and plastic-wrapped ice treats to ice cream in cardboard cups. The school also encouraged students to bring 'nude food' lunch boxes.

'I was amazed by the number of students who really jumped on board, especially with the single-use plastic bags,' Liz remembers.

It isn't just the students who learn. After hearing a Plastic Free July talk, teachers at Perth's Scotch College realised how much plastic was used to deliver their lunches in individual portions every day. Staff decided to purchase reusable plates and utensils and organised with the caterer to change the delivery model. The changes went beyond reducing their plastic waste.

'When we had the lunches delivered individually in plastic, staff tended to take their lunch back into the office and eat at their desks,' former teacher Chris Menage says. 'Switching to self-serve and reusable plates resulted in people sitting together in the lunch room and taking time out, so we benefited from having more conversations. It also meant there was less food waste as teachers could just serve as much as they wanted. In the long run this was a positive in terms of our catering contract.'

STUDENTS RISE TO THE CHALLENGE

Whangarei Primary School, New Zealand

After discovering just how much plastic was in students' lunch boxes, the school decided to make beeswax wraps as an eco-friendly alternative. The kids 'loved the whole process and what's even better is that they are using them!'

John XXIII College and Scotch College, Australia

The schools encouraged critical thought and reasoned arguments into plastics through debating the topics 'Plastic should be banned from school canteens' and 'Plastic should never have been invented'.

Levi Hildebrand and Leah Tidey, University of Victoria, Canada

Canadian university students Levi Hildebrand and Leah Tidey entered the City of Victoria's BYO Bag video competition with an entry showcasing alternatives to plastic bags. Using their $500 winnings, they organised a Plastic Free July beach clean-up on the Gorge Waterway, Vancouver Island, with the organisation Surfrider Foundation Vancouver Island. Participants collected 450 kilograms of litter.

Loyola University Chicago, USA

Students raised awareness of plastic straws on campus by making handmade signs using the tagline: *'It's just one plastic straw,' said 7.6 billion people.*

Kamla Nehru Public School, India
Students learned about the problems of plastic, and made posters and videos to spread the message and encourage people to use fewer plastic bags.

Keira Jack, Teddington School, UK
Following a nationwide competition for UK schools to raise awareness and help reduce plastic, student Keira Jack won with her design of an angler fish sculpture made from single-use plastic bottles. Her winning design was brought to life as a full-size sculpture and displayed in London during Plastic Free July.

The challenge caught on for students of all ages. Children at a family day-care centre in Australia wrapped reusable coffee cups with portraits of their dads for Father's Day, students from schools in Kenya and the United Arab Emirates pledged to refuse or reduce single-use plastics, and Bathurst students raised awareness by dancing to a rap written by a Sister of Mercy:

> I still have hope that the day is getting nearer
> When plastic packaging that we can't see clearer
> Becomes just a remnant of a bygone era
> Our generation is the one to care ...
> Win the war on dumb plastic everywhere.

These are just a handful of the incredible stories we've received from students and teachers all over the world. These initiatives give me hope for the future.

Change where you work

Single-use plastics in workplaces large and small have also been tackled by people inspired by Plastic Free July. It often starts with one person. This was the case with Rachel Shields, whose ideas for simple substitutions in the hospital where she worked managed to save tens of thousands of plastic cups from going into landfill each year.

Along with patients and colleagues at her hospital, Rachel was increasingly uneasy about the damage plastic was having on the environment. She saw a huge opportunity to reduce the hospital's reliance on plastic with some relatively simple changes.

'We started with the kiosk and catering service,' Rachel says, 'replacing plastic cups and utensils with wooden popsicle sticks and ceramic cups.'

By researching the solutions first, Rachel was able to present hospital management with straightforward substitutions. Along with catering supplies, plastic medication cups were replaced with paper alternatives, resulting in the hospital reducing their contribution to plastic landfill by a whopping 70 000 cups each year.

Going global

Sharing Plastic Free July stories from around the world became an important way to recognise people's efforts, inspire others to join and help them get started. The way the challenge played out in Perth, and even nationally, was just part of how it was unfolding. The stories reflected the diversity of people, the challenges they faced, and their community-specific actions.

It was impossible for us to provide advice and support to participants in other countries as the challenge grew, so it was a relief when people began contacting us to set up local groups to do this. They could translate our resources into local languages, run events and share information on where to source plastic-free alternatives. For example, in 2014 Jerry Biret set up the Plastic Free July Tahiti group, and engaged locals and tourists with French-language versions of resources. It was fantastic to work with groups like Jerry's that are spreading the challenge further than our resources could ever reach.

Here are just some of the initiatives from around the world that I have come across.

Sarah Rhodes, Cambodia

In the city of Siem Reap, Cambodia, Sarah Rhodes set up the Plastic Free Cambodia group in 2015 and worked with tourism operators, the hospitality industry and residents with the aim of reducing plastic litter.

Plastic Free July was the springboard that allowed people to start tackling the plastic problem, Sarah says – and she has seen the changes herself. 'Since 2015 the awareness of the topic in Cambodia has completely changed, especially amongst youth, people in the tourism sector and those living close to the cities. The amount of projects, businesses and NGOs with a focus on plastic reduction, environment and natural products is starting to bloom incredibly,' she says.

'There's still a lot more to do as things shift; with more knowledge comes more questions. We're now addressing topics such as recycling and bioplastics at a new and more informed level than any of the conversations taking place back in 2014. Then it was a once-a-year thing; now you will see groups out almost daily cleaning their city.'

Following their efforts, seeing images of people wearing green 'Plastic Free Cambodia' T-shirts with our turtle logo at events, and finding materials translated into Khmer language gave us hope that the 'reduce' message was making its way across many boundaries.

Vandana K, India

It was easy to find images of plastic pollution from all around the world but finding pictures of people being part of the solution was more challenging. Knowing her background in media, in 2018 I asked Vandana K from New Delhi for some help and she arranged to do a photo shoot of people in her community using reusables in their everyday lives. Vandana was able to capture images of people using their baskets at the community bazaars and filling water bottles. The way these images connected with others was so heartening. After sharing the photos on social media we saw a threefold increase in the number of people in India participating in Plastic Free July.

Vandana expressed how happy this made her. 'People have written to me and said, "I've been looking at [this movement] online and all these Western women, usually white, and I think, *I can't afford those things they are buying and I can't live the lifestyle of someone in New York.* But then I saw you and thought, *That's totally doable.*"'

Nick Morrison, New Zealand

Nick's football (soccer) team in New Zealand has taken the 'reduce plastic' message to the field. 'I felt the need to speak out. I feel a responsibility,' says Nick. 'In our team we have a fine system, so it's a $2 fine for things like being hungover or not turning up for training. It helps create a culture. Now there's a fine on using tape' – that is, the disposable tape used to hold shin pads in place, or to secure socks. The team instead use reusable elastic.

They've also stopped bringing single-use plastic bottles of sports drink. Instead, Nick buys a big tub of powder and has given the team their own reusable bottles. At first the changes seemed a bit unusual to his teammates, but now they're just accepted. When a new player starts and brings along his shin tape, the team says, 'No tape here, mate.'

Sonal Nayak, India

Changes shared from around the globe have always kept our momentum going. Sonal Nayak from India was married during Plastic Free July and opted for cardboard boxes to give gifts of sweets to the guests. 'We expected 1200 guests – I know, a big fat Indian wedding – and saved 1200 plastic containers, lids and stickers.'

Ministry of Tourism, Saint Kitts and Nevis

On the islands of Saint Kitts and Nevis in the Caribbean, local efforts to reduce single-use plastics drove wider uptake of the challenge. Residents and visitors were encouraged to forgo plastic straws and bring their own bags, and participating businesses provided bags and straws only when requested.

Buoyed by the exceptional feedback, support and cooperation during Plastic Free July 2017 and 2018, the local tourism ministry announced an initiative declaring 2019 'A plastic free year – a wave of change'. Dedicated events included movie screenings, releases of rehabilitated sea turtles, and youth activities during summer camps. The islands' plastic-free participants also held a march for a plastic-free Saint Kitts and Nevis at the end of July. It was a vibrant and inspiring event, with people displaying colourful homemade banners with messages of change.

> 'We are now beginning to see changes taking place around the two islands and for that we are most grateful. Of course, we still have work to do and we will continue to do it so that our people are more aware and educated.'
>
> – Diannille Taylor-Williams, coordinator of plastic-free initiatives, Ministry of Tourism, Saint Kitts and Nevis

Ben Lecomte, North Pacific Ocean

In June 2019, long-distance swimmer Ben Lecomte set off on his Vortex Swim through some of the most polluted parts of the North Pacific Ocean, including the 'Great Pacific Garbage Patch', to raise awareness of plastic pollution. With him was a support boat with ten crew members, who collected and researched marine debris along the way. They also joined the plastic-free challenge themselves – no mean feat when provisioning a boat for months at sea.

Ben has promoted Plastic Free July to his social media followers including a photo of him holding an underwater sign and via interviews around the world. It is an ongoing way for him to show his commitment and be part of the solution to the plastic pollution problem.

Mariska Nell, United Arab Emirates

In the UAE, a lot of people use single-use plastic water bottles for their daily drinking water. During Plastic Free July, information-sharing events included a quiz night, and a panel discussion about plastic waste solutions with hospitality industry experts.

'Many who attended the events started telling us of the changes that they were making. The swapping of single-use plastic bottles for filtered tap water was a big one, reducing potentially thousands of single-use bottles from being used,' Mariska says.

'Plastic Free July is merely the drop that starts the ripple effect of change throughout the year – not only in your community, but everywhere you go.'

Sora Cordonnier, Poland

Sora organised a Clean-Up Thursday public event to clean Las Wolski, the largest green space in Kraków – an area she describes as

> 'Once we are aware of issues, it is easier to make changes and if you are taking on a challenge with many people, it is easier to hold each other accountable and create team spirit.'
>
> – Mariska Nell, Plastic Free July event coordinator, United Arab Emirates

'more than worth saving'. The event invited people to gather together in the forest and restore the natural environment by collecting litter.

'We managed to collect around half a tonne of trash. There was everything from plastic bottles through to a washing machine,' Sora says. Many small acts make a difference and Sora hopes the forest will be 'a cleaner and more pleasant space for people to spend their time in'.

Irana Hawkins, USA

On an Alaska Airlines flight, Irana was chatting to a flight attendant, who noticed her durable stainless-steel cup. She said to Irana, 'Do you know it's Plastic Free July?'

'Amen,' Irana says, reporting this back to me. 'It's amazing that your campaign was mentioned by an Alaska Airlines flight attendant during a random conversation about my lifestyle behaviours. It's a slow haul but we're making progress towards the healthy planet we need to see.'

Josh and Alicia Bulbeck, UK

In 2018, Josh and Alicia Bulbeck did Plastic Free July and found forgoing single-use plastic for a month was harder than they expected, even in a city as large as London. Sourcing alternatives proved challenging, but instead of being disheartened, Plastic Free July acted as a catalyst for the couple to start a business.

'To our surprise the challenge turned out to be a daily uphill struggle and we realised we couldn't be the only ones in the UK who felt this way,' Alicia says. 'This is when we decided to act and created Zéro.' The store sells unpackaged food products and plastic-free accessories to help others to reduce their single-use plastic footprint.

•

After the Plastic Free July basket of cups photo went viral for Emu Point Cafe, Kate Marwick set up the Cup Exchange initiative in 2018 so people from all over the world could get involved. Customers have driven the growth in café participation, with some even 'dobbing in' their local café. Visiting Dunedin in New Zealand, I was delighted to see how many cafés that had their own basket of cups, each one as unique as the café itself.

Over 4400 cafés have now become Responsible Cafes, another Australian initiative that started in 2013. This group conducted weekly beach clean-ups but wanted to tackle the issue by reducing plastic waste at the source.

At the time of writing, 1040 Boomerang Bags communities around the world have sewed and distributed 462 650 shopping bags from donated fabrics. The initiative started in 2013 during a conversation about plastic pollution between two friends, Tania Potts and Jordyn de Boer, in Burleigh Heads, Queensland. 'Boomerang Bags fosters sustainable behaviour, one connection, one conversation, one bag at a time,' says Tania.

In 2019 Gabrielle Grime and her young family travelled around Australia. One of their stops was the remote South Australian town of Arno Bay, on the Eyre Peninsula, with a population of just 300 people.

'Outside the café was a sign saying *Plastic Free July*,' Gabrielle says. 'I thought it was fantastic. It was in the middle of nowhere.'

8

Momentum builds and the movement grows

With the stunning blue vista of Sydney Harbour behind me, feeling refreshed after a ferry ride from Circular Quay, I travelled by cable car to meet staff at Taronga Zoo. Visiting any zoo was a novelty to me and not something I'd experienced as a child. From my treetop vantage point, I saw an expanse of greenery and animals roaming spacious enclosures. A baby elephant wallowed in a mud bath.

It gave me such a rush to be there. I had discovered that the zoo participated in Plastic Free July, and was visiting to learn more about their efforts to reduce plastic.

Arriving early at the Forage and Graze café gave me a chance to observe some of the initiatives Taronga Zoo had taken. I noticed the absence of any litter, and the colourful covered bins clearly demarcated for general waste, food packaging and beverage containers. Inside the café's display cabinet, food was minimally wrapped in paper; there were bulk dispensers for sauces, reusable utensils, and self-serve salt and pepper.

Although the zoo's central purpose is animal conservation, climate change is a key environmental concern, and plastics are a big focus. 'It's part of the big picture,' says Rachael McAdam, Taronga's partnerships account manager. 'People like to focus on plastic because it's visual.'

As a fairly new staff member at Taronga, one of the first things Rachael noticed when she started working at the zoo was the very strong plastic-free culture. 'Using it was almost taboo,' she says. 'Staff use their own cups at the café and it is embraced by middle and senior management. We've done a lot around Plastic Free July … It hasn't just had an environmental impact – socially, it brings staff together.'

The plastic-free ethos at the zoo can be observed at all levels of the zoo's operations. The message is communicated to young visitors through the use of animal images with the logo 'Be Plastic Free for Me', vividly linking plastic to its effects on wildlife. Taronga Zoo's conservation programs have to respond to these impacts; the plight of Andrew the green sea turtle revealed how a turtle's first-ever journey could be impacted by marine debris. Andrew was found as an immobile hatchling and sent to Taronga Zoo. His rehabilitation showed that at just three weeks old he'd already ingested plastic. Thankfully Andrew was one of the lucky ones and he's since been returned to the wild with a tracker so his ongoing journey can be monitored. His story is shared as part of Taronga Zoo's Litter Free Oceans initiative for businesses and schools.

The zoo's efforts to reduce single-use plastics have also led to flow-on effects for external providers. They have invested time in working with contractors. The high visitor numbers mean that zoo staff have an opportunity to work with big companies and have some influence over their suppliers.

Compostable packaging material used at the zoo is mixed with animal waste and sent to an industrial composting facility. There are also reverse vending machines by the front entrance, part of the New South Wales Government's recently introduced container deposit scheme. The local community have returned 2 million beverage containers for recycling in the first two years of its operation.

A groundswell of change

There's a point where the energy from many acts or events combines to create significant change. Just as streams join together to become rivers, so the impetus from individuals all over the world flows into larger systems to create global change. Looking back, it was after the fifth Plastic Free July challenge in 2015 that awareness and engagement in the plastic waste problem really started to gain that worldwide momentum.

People were paying attention. News of plastics being found inside animals, our food and seemingly everywhere on Earth became alarmingly frequent. Organisations like ours that were working on the plastic waste issue were finally starting to get traction. There were many people involved and many diverse approaches in making this happen.

It was August 2015 when the disturbing video from Costa Rica of turtle researchers removing a plastic straw from a sea turtle's nostril went viral. It wasn't just spread via environmental organisations; I had countless people tell me how distressing they had found the video. To this day I still can't bring myself to watch the clip. It's one thing to see plastic in dead animals but there is a heightened level of distress and helplessness involved in watching an animal suffer.

The images continued. The documentary film *A Plastic Ocean* was released in 2016 and the following year the final episode of the BBC's *Blue Planet II*, narrated and presented by Sir David Attenborough, focused on the impact of plastics on marine organisms and implored viewers to start reversing those impacts by reducing their plastic use. Even if we weren't yet encountering plastic's devastating environmental effects firsthand, we were witnessing the damage on our screens. It was only a matter of looking up from those screens to make the connection: plastic was intrinsic to our daily lives. We could not separate our reliance on it from its ultimate effect on our fragile ecosystems.

This growing awareness of the issue was highlighted in other ways. Our language and attitudes became more sophisticated: 'waste' was increasingly referred to as a 'resource' and the 'Three R's' grew to include other important words such as refuse, rethink, repair, repurpose and rot (compost).

'Single-use' plastic was a difficult concept to communicate in 2011, but in 2018 the term was selected, out of a possible 4.5 billion words, as the *Collins Dictionary* word of the year. This was attributed to the sharing of images of wildlife encountering plastics, bans on single-use plastic items and global reduction campaigns. At the time, Collins reported that 'the word has seen a four-fold increase in usage since 2013'.

The increased awareness was reflected in the remarkable spread and growth of Plastic Free July. Every day, in a multitude of ways, people continued to reduce their plastic. The ideas filtered through local communities to businesses and larger corporations that were able to make changes on a much broader scale. When those influences combined, the movement felt like a living ecosystem with a diversity of entities allowing it to thrive.

Regardless of the original impetus or the entry point to reducing plastic waste, any positive action around reduction converges with other actions to build momentum.

Seeing efforts in action

Over the years, much of what I've learned about making changes at scale has come from conversations and from seeing efforts firsthand. When we share these stories of solutions through Plastic Free July, they allow people to go beyond the headlines and statistics and to learn what others have done. It is immensely valuable to know the steps others have taken and the challenges they have overcome. So, as the impetus around the plastics issues grew, it seemed more important than ever to connect.

When I visited places like Taronga Zoo and saw the growth of initiatives, it gave me immense hope. Knowing so many others were working on the issue spurred me on, and provided many opportunities to learn and collaborate including my 2016 Churchill Fellowship exploring solutions to the plastic pollution problem. For me, doing on-the-ground research and having conversations made a far greater impression and was far more useful than trying to tackle plastics through secondary resources.

Travelling from Hong Kong to the US and Europe, the Fellowship gave me an opportunity to observe the problem and solutions firsthand as I met with local groups doing clean-ups everywhere from an island in Hong Kong Harbour and a remote beach in Hawaii to a stand-up paddleboard clean-up in a London canal. Many of these groups were already participating in Plastic Free July and used the campaign as a practical way to engage local communities. In each country I linked up with not-for-profits and government agencies, and the knowledge I gained from their initiatives added another piece to the puzzle that we could then share with Plastic Free July participants.

In a café in Oakland, California, Samantha Sommer chatted to me about the cultural shift involved in the ReThink Disposable initiative in the San Francisco Bay area. The campaign's team zeroed in on high impact trash areas to minimise the use of single-use products and offered free assistance to food service businesses to reduce disposable packaging. As part of the initiative, they developed comprehensive case studies including cost–benefit analyses, which demonstrated that businesses were saving money by switching to reusables. This was a really important part of the learning curve for me, because often economics and the environment are seen as an either/or consideration; there is still a widespread belief that being environmentally responsible, for example taking action to reduce single-use plastics, is not economically viable. In fact, this is not always the case, particularly when we look at the long-term economic benefits of waste reduction. For example, the ReThink Disposable initiative reported that its 244 participating businesses reduced disposable packaging by almost 25 million items annually, saving an estimated US$760 000 in the longer term.

In Amsterdam, I cycled to the offices of the Plastic Soup Foundation with Michiel Roscam Abbing and absorbed details of their Beat the Microbead campaign, which lobbied businesses and governments and raised consumer awareness about plastic microbeads in personal care products. A highlight of this initiative was the introduction of the Zero Plastic Inside logo, making it easier for consumers to buy cosmetics with confidence. That three-pronged attack of education, making alternatives readily identifiable and working with key players, has been really instructive for Plastic Free July.

Connecting the dots

These experiences were just a few of the dozens of initiatives I discovered during my Fellowship and I have shared them widely since – not just with our participants but with other groups and regulators. Many more of them appear throughout this book. Through these connections people have been able to reach out to enterprises from around the world, take part in their initiatives and adapt solutions to plastic concerns in their own communities.

Even in this digitally connected world, however, I was often surprised by the lack of awareness and connection between organisations which could sometimes result in a duplication of effort and initiatives. By the end of my trip I had installed six different litter-recording apps on my smartphone. Each had been developed by a separate group for their own purposes, but there were so many different options with information stored in different data sets. The disparate data made it difficult to try to get a picture of the litter issue if you wanted to collate all the information for a particular item or area.

On a positive note, by using and sharing these resources through Plastic Free July we could point participants to existing initiatives to better support their efforts. I often used the Beat the Microbead app to scan barcodes of supermarket products and posted pictures of those containing plastic microbeads on social media. A number of not-for-profits including the Plastic Pollution Coalition also support and share the Plastic Free July campaign challenge, with CEO and co-founder Dianna Cohen saying that collaboration 'helped build, catalyse and spawn the international movement to refuse single-use plastic'. 'Starting from a focus on the month of July and expanding to all the months in a year, year after year, we work in concert towards a world free of plastic pollution,' Dianna says.

Connecting with passionate people around the world created a supportive network that I still work with today – the whole is definitely greater than the sum of the parts.

A fresh approach for Plastic Free July

I returned from the Churchill Fellowship with a head full of ideas, invigorated by the incredible initiatives taking place in an expanded global network of single-use plastic free advocates. It marked the start of a new phase for Plastic Free July, and a revitalised plan that involved:

- shifting the focus of plastic pollution from an oceans issue to a problem that starts upstream, in our daily lives
- collaborating by sharing resources and data
- sharing stories of solutions to amplify impacts
- using tools for individual behaviour change to direct actions upstream and influence government and business.

I realised that Plastic Free July was unique: it was an annual challenge that anyone, anywhere in the world, could sign up for to get started on their path to avoiding single-use plastics. The overwhelming feedback was that people had found it was a valuable way to start conversations and initiate change in their communities.

A lot of the attraction was that despite the Plastic Free July title, the 'ask' was for people to do just one thing. That made it achievable for everyone. Knowing that people were doing the challenge wasn't the same as knowing if it had *impact*, though. At the end of the day, was Plastic Free July making a difference by reducing plastic waste? And, if it was, how could we take the next steps and reach a wider audience so we could start a shift in consumer demand, leading to far-reaching changes in business and government?

Changing our behaviour at the source

Despite knowing where we wanted to take the plastic-free challenge, we didn't know how to get there, and we needed to add some skills and resources to our team. I'd heard of the work of behavioural economist Colin Ashton-Graham, and we engaged him to initiate an evidence-based approach using insights from behavioural science. Colin develops insights into the way we make choices and applies these insights to enable behaviour change for sustainability.

Behavioural economics draws upon psychology to try to explain why people make seemingly irrational choices such as taking more risk, opting for a deal that will cost them more, buying things that they have no use for or damaging an environment that they care for. Practitioners then turn this research into behavioural insights that can help to influence behaviours.

To harness the power of behavioural insights, we started with research. The first step was general public surveys in Western Australia to really understand people's attitudes to plastic waste, and to find out what their current behaviours and choices as consumers were. Our surveys showed that although there was a shared community value around not wasting resources, this was disconnected from people's actual behaviours in terms of plastic consumption:

- 84 per cent of survey respondents were concerned with plastics ending up in landfill
- 94 per cent of survey respondents agreed that 'plastic pollution in the ocean is a big problem'
- yet only 50 per cent of respondents chose to avoid single-use plastics such as disposable cups, straws and bags.

Through this research, we were able to identify the behaviour changes that would be most effective to target in our campaign – these were the ones that people would be most likely to adopt and result in real reductions in littering, waste and resource consumption. Understanding these in detail gave us a real opportunity to build an online communications toolbox including case studies, an 'action picker' that listed ideas, and other resources including badges and posters.

Doing this work made me realise just how much of a bubble I lived and worked in, and how our approach was limited in terms of reaching people. Instead of testing the new resources on my colleagues, friends and volunteers, Colin designed a structured survey to test them on the streets and in the Perth CBD, away from the eco-friendly suburb of Fremantle where I live. It was an eye-opener. What I had thought was clear and informative actually included far too much information and people didn't immediately understand the 'ask'.

In the end, we made the posters about the challenge, and about bags, cups, straws and takeaway containers, clearer and simpler. An

THE BEHAVIOURAL INSIGHTS TOOLBOX

Behavioural insights offer tools that can help people make behaviour changes for sustainability, including:

- *framing* to help people give precedence to the environment
- *interrupting* habitual behaviours to make room for a new choice
- *norms* to help people feel confident about adopting a new behaviour
- *nudges* to prompt a decision
- providing *feedback* to magnify behaviours with long-term consequences.

editable version allowed people to add their own initiatives and logos, and everything was open source; anyone, from an individual to a business owner, could download and print them or display them in a workplace. The poster for shopping bags didn't have a picture of suffering wildlife or a plastic bag with a red line through it and a 'SAY NO' message – a strategy that our research showed to have limited appeal, restricted to activists or people who were already aware. Instead, an illustration of a reusable shopping bag and a cardboard box showed people what we were asking them to do. The strategy was simple: build on the existing concern by adding the polite ask:

> Communities around the globe are concerned about plastic ending up in landfill and polluting the oceans … that's why 1 million people are choosing to be part of Plastic Free July. Please join our effort to help the environment.

> Choose to refuse plastic shopping bags: bring your own bag or use a box.

At the bottom of each poster, we listed the key motivators for change we'd identified, which took the problem beyond just being an oceans issue and allowed people to select their own motivation for action:

> Avoid Landfill Waste, Reduce your Eco-footprint, Protect the Ocean.

Plastic Free July's 'Choose to refuse plastic shopping bags' poster

'It is the actions of many that will establish the norms and community expectations that drive social change. The challenge is to nudge the visible changes that embody a more sustainable future.'

– Colin Ashton-Graham, behavioural economist

We chose to use illustrations for a more universal appeal; photographs would be less relatable. It was a lot of work for what was such a simple end result but it worked. It wasn't long before the resources were being downloaded, adapted and shared around the world. Some participants such as Kirsty Symmons in Kelowna, British Columbia, Canada, got businesses around the city to participate and shared photos of store owners holding up posters on a 'Plastic Free July Kelowna' Facebook page. It was so heartening to see our resources translated into other languages, too, and really satisfying to know they were useful. I was grateful for the people who took the time to adapt them to suit their needs. With my Spanish heritage I was especially delighted to see the efforts of a group of women from the social enterprise Life Out Of Plastic (L.O.O.P.) in Lima, Peru, who shared all our posters in Spanish, where the ask became *¿Te unes al desafío?* – 'Will you join the challenge?'

The Plastic Free Foundation

Although Plastic Free July had spread beyond our council boundaries by the second year of the challenge, it wasn't until 2017, when we did our first survey of the Western Australian general public to measure awareness and participation, that we realised just how big it had become. As we suspected, the survey revealed that only a small percentage of participants had actually formally signed on for the challenge so, although 15 000 people and organisations had registered

PLASTIC FREE JULY

The redesigned and simplified Plastic Free July logo, designed by Media on Mars (2019)

for Plastic Free July 2016, an estimated 1 million people had taken part. It was a staggering number for me to get my head around.

For a few years I had been doing much of the work running Plastic Free July nationally and internationally in my own time – it was only one of the projects I worked on in my part-time role as a waste educator at the Western Metropolitan Regional Council, but it was the one I was most passionate about. At the end of 2017, it was time to leap into the next phase. With the support of the council, I left to set up the Plastic Free Foundation as an independent charity to continue delivering the Plastic Free July challenge, to better support participants around the world and to increase our impact.

Setting up a not-for-profit (or 'for-purpose', as we prefer to say) has been another steep learning curve but definitely a worthwhile one. Since our vision is for a world without plastic waste, we often think about what that might look like. It is also what inspires our actions on how we might get there. Plastic Free July is still based in

> 'The Plastic Free Foundation is out there as an advocate, helping us – not using a big-stick approach, but talking to the community about how, together, we might reduce the amount of single-use plastic that we use. They are committed to working in collaboration with people, giving them ideas and the how-to, so that together we can make a change and reduce our footprint.'
>
> – WA Environment Minister Stephen Dawson

Perth but operating across the globe with a small but passionate team of part-time staff and volunteers who work from home offices, cafés and co-working spaces, generously supported by pro bono service providers and, more recently, grants from the Western Australian state government.

Business gets on board

True to the grassroots origin of the challenge, the community approach and uptake has continued among everyone who has worked on the campaign and supported the Foundation. It is really gratifying to see the changes they have made in their lives and workplaces. Staff from corporate partners, as well as funding agencies Lotterywest and the WA Department of Water and Environmental Regulation, have invited me to speak at their plastic-free morning teas or 'lunch and learn' sessions that are often live-streamed to offices around the country and overseas.

The reach of Plastic Free July has extended to business leaders who then influence and encourage others. At the Perth offices of our legal partner Herbert Smith Freehills, a number of initiatives to avoid plastic waste have been implemented since staff were exposed to the challenge.

'Our staff response has been overwhelmingly positive,' says partner Dan Dragovic. 'They love the fact that they are part of an organisation that is doing things and also encouraging them to do things at work and at home.' With 200 staff in the Perth office and over 5000 globally, the firm sees the potential for each small change they make to have a big impact across the business.

Employees from KeepCup, the Melbourne-based company making barista-standard reusable cups for over a decade, already had a culture of avoiding single-use plastics such as coffee cups, water

BUSINESS LEADERS MAKING A DIFFERENCE

Lendlease

Barangaroo South precinct, Sydney

When I set up Plastic Free July as a not-for-profit, I knew I wanted to take it to the next level, so it was fortunate that around the same time I was in the conference audience when Lendlease's Lucy Sharman – the company's sustainability manager – gave a talk about their development of the Barangaroo South precinct in Sydney's Darling Harbour. Lendlease is a multinational construction and development company, and Barangaroo South is one of Australia's most significant urban redevelopment projects. During Lucy's talk, I was struck by the sustainability efforts that the company had made during the project.

Lucy had already been personally involved with Plastic Free July, and she wanted to take the 'reduce' message into her workplace and across the Barangaroo precinct. On that scale, there was scope to make massive changes. Lendlease was already making inroads to reduce waste, with advanced systems to manage their waste and maximise recycling streams to reduce landfill. When I toured these facilities with Lucy, I was excited to brainstorm ways we could get Plastic Free July involved to encourage behaviour change around avoiding waste. It was an opportunity to take the message to a much wider audience.

An offer by Lendlease to host the launch of the Plastic Free Foundation allowed us to hold the event in Sydney in 2018. It was an opportunity for other Barangaroo South tenants to find out about Plastic Free July, and for participating organisations and networks in Sydney to join together. At that point, most people still didn't really know who was behind the Plastic Free July challenge, or where and how it had all started. Many presumed it had begun on the east coast of Australia or in the US.

Barangaroo takes the challenge

Designed for 23 000 office workers, the Barangaroo International Towers are home to many national and global firms, so it was a really exciting opportunity for Plastic Free July. For Lucy, it was about getting her organisation and other tenants on board. The launch took place six weeks before 1 July, and the uptake of the challenge surprised us all. The idea of being part of a global movement to reduce single-use plastics appealed to the employees. The plastic pollution problem was very topical and the businesses were able to make changes that were overwhelmingly supported by employees; it helped that Plastic Free July was an independent initiative.

Tarah Spencer, Lendlease's national community manager within the corporate real estate division, was at the launch and became a big driver. 'I was bitten by the Plastic Free July bug,' she says. 'I knew that there was a huge opportunity for us to make a difference, firstly in our office here at Barangaroo and then around Australia.'

By July, Tarah, Lucy and the team had developed a full program to activate Plastic Free July in the workplace, including events such as guest speakers, lunchtime learning sessions for things like making beeswax wraps and cleaning products, movie screenings and pop-up market days. The message was communicated to all employees and other Barangaroo tenants.

Company-wide initiatives

In the meantime, the challenge quickly flowed through to other operational areas at Lendlease. Tarah and Lucy worked with their internal café to completely eliminate disposable cups and straws and provided staff with reusable glass cups for takeaway coffees, avoiding 6000 disposable cups in that month alone – and every month since. Procurement changes sometimes meant working with suppliers to change processes if existing ones couldn't accommodate their plastic-free supply needs. Plastic-wrapped pens in the stationery cupboards were phased out, as were individual plastic-wrapped tea bags in the kitchens. The changes weren't always easy, with one supplier originally offering to unwrap each item before delivery; Lendlease instead worked with this supplier to change their processes.

What difference can one person make? Lucy Sharman's personal convictions and actions by taking on the Plastic Free July challenge now reach all of the commercial and residential tenants at Barangaroo South. The sustainability measures she has helped implement flow through to thousands of people every day.

bottles, bags and straws, but sponsoring the Plastic Free Foundation in 2019 saw them increase their efforts.

For KeepCup co-founder and managing director Abigail Forsyth, Plastic Free July was an opportunity to 'go deeper' on the single-use plastic-free journey. The company organised fruit for staff to 'shift snacking away from packaged treats', bought office milk in reusable glass bottles and supplied communal bread bags to avoid single-use paper packaging from the local bakery.

'As leaders of the business community, I think we've got a responsibility to show each other the way.'

– Dan Dragovic, partner, Herbert Smith Freehills

'Plastic Free July brought our teams together for communal lunches in our Melbourne, London and Los Angeles offices. It sparked great conversations with customers and suppliers, but also in our homes, about the challenges and opportunities of living single-use free,' Abigail says.

Our website and rebranding team also got on board. After redesigning Plastic Free July's website, staff from design agency Media on Mars went on to deliver our posters to local cafés and the exposure led to changes in their own lives.

'Working on the Plastic Free July campaign and the website totally opened my eyes,' website developer Roman Karachevtsev says. 'I try to use less plastic. We try not to buy any fruit wrapped in plastic and we have tried to cut down on the [single-use plastics] we use every day.'

These are typical of the stories regularly shared with me. Knowing there are even more initiatives out there continues to give the Foundation the momentum we need to keep making inroads at all levels.

From engaging staff to participate in the challenge to improving recycling, reducing single-use plastics in procurement and operations, to helping customers to use reusables – there is such a variety of ways that businesses have taken on the challenge to reduce plastic waste.

Plastic-free food service

In our food systems, the single-use plastics that we see in packaging, food serviceware and takeaway containers are just the tip of the iceberg. Behind the scenes, single-use plastics are widely used in kitchens for meal preparation and storage, food delivery and transport, and extensively in agriculture – in everything from mulching to bale-wrap and storage of grains and fertilisers. Making changes in the food industry involves adapting systems, working with suppliers and educating customers.

At Bread in Common, a local restaurant in Fremantle, waste reduction efforts were visible to me as a customer. For a start, the sparkling water is made on site, avoiding the bottled water usually transported from overseas. I asked co-owner and chef Scott Brannigan about what they did in the kitchen and he chatted about how they grow a lot of their own vegetables, have food scraps composted, and have meat and seafood delivered in plastic tubs that are then washed, sterilised and collected with the next delivery – avoiding the disposable polystyrene (foam) boxes.

'It just took a little bit of discipline, and time to get my staff to believe this is better,' Scott says. 'Now they are all on board and it's just what we do. We've got efficient at it, and it saves time as we don't have to cut open plastic ties and bags and throw them away.'

There are cost savings too, he points out. 'It also probably saves suppliers money in the long run because they avoid the packaging. Now they ask other restaurants if they are interested in doing it too. I'm just doing something little but it will make a difference, rather than doing nothing.'

Scott was inspired to make changes for the benefit of his young daughters. He looked at all the waste in his bin and it made him ponder those same questions I had when I started this journey.

'I wondered where it was going to go and what would happen to it, and if there was a way of making it better. I don't want to wreck the world for them. I want to make our impact as low as possible, otherwise they will have to fix our muck-ups.'

At the new restaurant he is setting up, Scott is taking his

waste-reduction efforts to the next level. He hasn't purchased a cryovac machine, which many restaurants use to vacuum-pack (in plastic) and cook food, and he is challenging his new chef to cook in other ways. In the kitchen, he uses reusable containers with lids to avoid plastic film.

Takeaway food is synonymous with plastic containers, but restaurants are finding ways around this. Taking his cue from takeaway delivery systems in Mumbai, Amritpal Singh Atwal, who owns Baba's Kitchen Indian restaurant in Seymour, Victoria, has implemented a system using stainless-steel lunch boxes or 'tiffins' as a response to the Plastic Free July initiative. The takeaway scheme operates through a deposit system and the customer feedback has been largely positive, with thousands of plastic items removed from this one restaurant each month.

Supermarkets play a huge role in either making it challenging to source plastic-free alternatives or else driving plastic reduction. Ainslie IGA in Canberra participated in Plastic Free July in 2019 with an exciting array of initiatives, displaying Plastic Free July's editable posters to promote the changes. The store had already offered cardboard boxes for years, but used Plastic Free July as a trial period to remove plastic bags altogether.

Store manager Dimitri Mihailakis sourced quality paper bags to minimise potential customer dissatisfaction, removed plastic cutlery from the deli, let people bring their own containers, and introduced a returnable and reusable container scheme. 'It all went way better than we could have hoped so we haven't looked back,' he says.

Dimitri also sourced plastic-free products and kept them on prominent display. 'At Ainslie IGA we are lucky to have such an informed and socially aware community to support us in initiatives like this. We are in a position to make a real difference and the constant reaffirmation by our clientele only pushes us to keep going.'

Supermarkets are able to implement these changes more readily

WHAT'S IN THAT TEA BAG?

By the time we got to this point of the book, Jo and I estimated we had consumed over 1600 cups of tea. Many people love their cuppas, but what isn't always known is that they often contain plastic.

Tea bags are made from several different materials: the bag, seal, tag and sometimes even a small staple. While tea bags were once made from natural fibres and could completely biodegrade, now many are made and sealed with plastic. To enjoy plastic-free tea:

- Buy loose leaf tea from a bulk food store, or purchase a brand that is packaged in a cardboard box without a plastic inner bag. Make your tea in a teapot and use a strainer, or try a tea infuser. Many people report this is a more economical way to drink tea and say they prefer the taste.
- If you want to find out if your favourite brand of tea bag is plastic-free, do a bit of internet research. Companies are now starting to make changes and the list of plastic-free brands is getting longer.
- For herbal alternatives, I use slices of ginger or fresh lemon verbena and lemongrass from the garden.

when supported by national brands, and those brands are responding to calls for plastic-free items. Australian tea company Nerada, for example, now sells loose-leaf tea in a recycled cardboard box with a fold-out pouring spout and no other internal packaging. In July 2019 they supported Plastic Free July, launching other loose-leaf tea ranges and also trialling tea bags made from 100 per cent natural fibres instead of the synthetic fibres used in many tea bags.

Cleaning up festivals and events

Music festivals and concerts are unifying events, where people come together in their shared appreciation of arts and culture. But over the years, the aftermath of these events – plastic-strewn fields, discarded plastic tarps and tents – has become disturbingly familiar. Single-use plastics are frequently used to serve food and drink, and the rubbish left behind impacts the environment. Cleaning up comes at a cost, and the public's perception of festival-goers plummets.

Fortunately, in more recent years we've started to see an increasing number of event managers take action to reduce plastic waste. In July 2017, a euphoric image appeared on Plastic Free July's Twitter feed. From the Santa Barbara Bowl in California beamed a photo of internationally acclaimed musician Jack Johnson with his stainless-steel pint cup held high. Behind him, the smiling crowd also raised their cups in the air. The message thrilled me:

> Jack & the crowd celebrate @plasticfreejuly @sbbowl. All fans received reusable pints to reduce single-use plastic!

Now an ambassador for the Plastic Free Foundation, Jack is adamant about the role the music industry can play in stemming the tide of plastic. 'A great first step is to commit to using reusable water bottles. I'm working with the music industry to reduce plastic waste through the BYOBottle campaign. Artists are teaming up with venues, festivals and fans to promote reusable bottles and water refill stations. Together we can turn the tide on plastic pollution.'

Two years later I happened to be visiting Santa Barbara and was delighted to see many of those same bright-blue cups still being put to use by concertgoers. People I spoke to said they used them at all concerts at the Santa Barbara Bowl and at any other opportunity. In that same year, even festivals as large as Glastonbury had joined

'Plastic Free July inspires me to step up my commitment to reducing single-use plastic in my daily life and on tour.'

– Jack Johnson, musician and Plastic Free Foundation ambassador

in, removing single-use water bottles and providing refill stations, removing over a million single-use plastic bottles from the festival.

Conferences are another example of large gatherings creating plastic waste. If you've been to one, you'll be all too familiar with the usual plastic line-up: name badges, plastic lanyards, packaged mints, sample bags, plastic water bottles and plastic utensils, to name just a few. Again, proactive conference organisers are working hard to bridge the disconnect between innovative presentations and the single-use plastic created by these events.

The organisers of the Australian Marine Sciences Association faced this dilemma with their annual marine conference held in Fremantle in 2019. Their solution was to forward plan and 'walk the talk' by organising a plastic-free conference for 570 attendees. The committee engaged an event organiser to help fill the brief and the result was an impressive array of alternatives including stiff cardboard name badges, bamboo lanyards, natural tote bags, encouraging participants to BYO reusable water bottles and coffee cups or use their returnable cups and glassware, and no packaged mints. Impressively, they didn't just manage to go plastic free – they did it without a budget increase.

Since the conference and follow-up media showcasing plastic-free alternatives, the event organisers have been approached by other conference planners seeking advice on how to reduce plastic waste at their events.

Around the world

Organisations of all types and sizes now participate in the Plastic Free July challenge. After all, single-use plastics are a material that almost everyone comes across every day, and with all the attention on the issue, Plastic Free July provides an opportunity to act. It has become an annual fixture on many corporate calendars. And there are so many solutions. Burlington Golf & Country Club in Canada, for example, shared on Twitter that for Plastic Free July they adapted the water fountains out on the course to make it easier for patrons to refill their bottles.

Even the biggest changes in businesses can often be traced back to individuals taking action. When the momentum pushes beyond the personal, it can create long-lasting change on a much bigger scale and influence internal business processes that then filter across partnerships, contractors and suppliers. If businesses make changes to their procurement policies, for example, it can have significant and far-reaching impacts, and when those impacts are multiplied they can profoundly change the system. I think it's important to reflect on this in the face of the often-asked question 'What difference can one person make?'

There have been countless ways that businesses have gotten involved, coming up with solutions that offer a blueprint for others inspired by their success. Here is a small taste of some of the diverse Plastic Free July initiatives from around the world.

Air New Zealand

In 2019, to mark Plastic Free July, Air New Zealand committed to almost double the number of single-use plastic items removed from its operations that year – nearly 55 million items. The airline also removed individual plastic water bottles from some services. This was

IDEAS FOR YOUR WORKPLACE

These ideas have worked for us, and may work for your workplace too.

1. Share Plastic Free July in your internal communications. Encourage staff to take the challenge together. Suggest realistic options and ways of getting there, e.g. 'Choose to refuse' and 'Switch *x* for *y*'.
2. Set up ideas as choices that give control to staff or customers, e.g. 'Consider bringing your own reusable water bottle to work, or choose to purchase one at front reception.'
3. Keep the 'ask' easy and achievable, e.g. putting up the Plastic Free July reusable cup poster in the staff room and by the door helps remind people to take their cups.
4. Include a purpose or outcome, not just an instruction, e.g. 'By using our water fountain to refill your bottle, you'll be helping us to reduce our single-use plastic bottle use. Last month we reduced our consumption by 600 bottles.'

estimated to divert more than 460 000 bottles from landfill for the year, as well as reduce carbon emissions by more than 300 000 kilograms per year by reducing aircraft weight.

'When sourcing viable substitutes for single-use plastic, we faced a number of hurdles; upstream we encountered limited low impact alternatives on the market, and downstream we found a lack of composting and recycling facilities in New Zealand to process packaging that was not made from fossil-fuel derived plastics,' says Air New Zealand's head of sustainability Lisa Daniell. 'We are eager to work with stakeholders across our supply chain to move more quickly towards a future that is not so reliant on plastics.'

One of the key drivers behind these changes was direct feedback to Air New Zealand from customers and employees that challenged the business's reliance on plastic. Air New Zealand then set up cross-functional teams to work out how to substitute a portion of the single-use plastics utilised in the business, and embarked on an employee engagement campaign that had positive results.

'Air New Zealand staff from around the globe met through internal social network Yammer to share how they were reducing their plastic footprint both at work and at home, with over a thousand ideas shared.'

Hostelling International, Norway

The Plastic Free July challenge was pivotal in significantly reducing single-use plastic through the Say HI to Sustainability project, an exchange partnership between non-profit organisations Hostelling International Norway, Hostelling International Brazil and the Norwegian Agency of Exchange Cooperation (Norec).

'We were able to ban most of the single-use plastic as well as replace single-use items,' sustainability exchange coordinator Emilia Barreto says. In two hostels out of their 43-hostel network, staff managed to avoid 19 050 plastic items in July alone, including plastic egg cups, spoons and coffee stirrers. These were replaced with porcelain egg cups, stainless-steel spoons and bamboo stirrers. 'This was a major accomplishment for us and definitely will inspire other hostels to follow this amazing initiative in the future,' says Emilia.

The project took a hands-on approach, where all staff were committed to suggestions around replacing plastic and single-use items. 'Their ideas were incorporated whenever possible and we were thrilled to see how people engaged in this initiative.'

Contimetra, Portugal

Sofia Sampaio took the Plastic Free July challenge into Contimetra, an industrial equipment supply company. In an effort to reduce plastic, staff were provided with personalised mugs and glass coffee cups. The company also shared multimedia presentations highlighting plastic waste issues and potential solutions.

Initially there was some resistance and a few complaints, but after a year 'the plastic cups are almost forgotten', Sofia says. 'We can proudly say that we have saved more than 9000 water cups, 12 000 coffee cups and 12 000 plastic stirrers in one year.'

Sands China, Macau

Almost 3000 team members from the resort developer and operator took the challenge and pledged plastic-free lifestyle changes. Some 28 000 staff were given reusable metal straws.

After 2019's challenge, director of sustainability Meridith Beaujean sent us this great message: 'July is over now but this is only the beginning! The enthusiasm and response to Plastic Free July from all Sands China Teams was amazing!'

Compari's On The Park, Michigan, USA

Some businesses have taken the challenge beyond reducing plastic waste and supported the work of the Foundation. Julia Hill, the events and catering manager at Compari's On The Park in Plymouth, Michigan, told us about their July Dine to Donate dinner.

'Fifteen per cent of every food bill was donated to the Plastic Free Foundation. For Plastic Free July we created a cocktail called "The Last Straw". Two dollars from each cocktail sold throughout the month was also donated.'

For Plastic Free July, Compari's transitioned from plastic straws to paper straws at all three of their restaurants. 'Plastic Free July has also inspired us to shift toward more sustainable packaging for [takeaway] orders. Looking forward to promoting Plastic Free July again next year and making even more improvements at all three restaurants!'

Zoos and aquariums

Around the world, participating in Plastic Free July is a popular choice for dozens of zoos and aquariums which, like Taronga Zoo, want to make a difference to reduce their plastic waste.

The World Association of Zoos and Aquariums (WAZA) is embracing the challenge head-on with a range of initiatives. WAZA has a global membership of 400 zoos and aquariums, and many are tackling the crisis in their supply chains and in initiatives for visitors. 'A number of WAZA members participate in the Plastic Free July challenge and at the same time encourage their visitors to participate as well,' says Martin Zordan, interim CEO. 'It's a fantastic initiative to challenge people to think about how they consume single-use plastics.'

SEA LIFE Sydney Aquarium replaced a tank of jellyfish with plastics that had been collected from Sydney Harbour. Zoos Victoria marked the start of Plastic Free July by blowing bubbles for their conservation program Bubbles Not Balloons, and asked the public to replace outdoor balloons with wildlife-friendly alternatives. Auckland Zoo installed free water stations to replace single-use plastic water bottles, and at the Two Oceans Aquarium in South Africa a month-long line-up in 2019 included clean-ups, activities and even interactive theatre to encourage young South Africans to create positive change.

The Two Oceans Aquarium staff witness the devastation caused by plastic firsthand, and raising awareness is a major part of their efforts. 'Our engagement with the Plastic Free July campaign began in earnest in 2016, and since then we have successfully built onto, and added value to, the enthusiastic local and global momentum each year,' says Two Oceans Aquarium environmental campaigner Hayley McLellan.

'We participate in Plastic Free July every year to further highlight the issue of plastic pollution. It's incredibly encouraging to see how the momentum has grown both locally and globally, and to see how packaging manufacturers, civil society, brands and governments are making the transition to plastic-free and reusable alternatives,' Hayley says.

Liz Zavodsky, executive director of EcoChallenge, based in Portland, Oregon in the US, contacted me when organising a Plastic Free July EcoChallenge in 2018 for 58 zoos and aquariums in North America.

'They wanted to embrace their conservation mission more and understand what plastics are doing to the planet,' Liz says. '[The staff] were concerned it's not just sea turtles affected by plastic but also land animals.' As zoos, she says 'They wanted to 'bring awareness to plastics'.

'Plastic Free July gave staff and their visitors something tangible they could do in their life, because people thought, "This is a huge issue and its overwhelming to me but knowing that I can make this change and it has this impact makes me feel better about my ability to make this change."'

'Thank you Plastic Free July for giving our lives more meaning. For a month we belonged to a community, bound by purpose to reduce plastic, focused on change and telling powerful stories. We can do better every month.'

– Dr Jenny Gray, CEO, Zoos Victoria

LAND OF THE QUOKKA JOINS IN

Rottnest Island Authority

Rottnest Island, Western Australia

Rottnest Island is an iconic holiday destination accessed by ferry from Perth. For visitors, it offers the chance to be at one with nature, with no cars and abundant wildlife. The island is well known for its native marsupial quokka population and the adorable quokka antics have gone viral thanks to celebrities posting 'quokka selfies' on social media.

Residents, businesses and visitors participated in Rottnest's first Plastic Free July challenge in 2016 led by the Rottnest Island Authority (RIA). Although the general store on the island hasn't used plastic bags for many years, the Plastic Free July challenge offered a unique opportunity for a broader approach to plastic reduction.

RIA's former environmental manager Holly Knight said the first year focused on straws, and although it wasn't always easy, they 'chipped away' over the years to the point where there is now a total plastic straw ban on the island.

'The arguments I had about straws!' Holly says. 'We were constantly picking up straws from the beaches. The challenge was a very tangible way to address plastic on the beach and hold businesses a bit more accountable.'

Seeing the results

On a small island, the impact of plastic reduction solutions on the environment is very noticeable. Rottnest has nesting wedge-tailed shearwaters that are 'particularly susceptible to plastic consumption'. 'We have a very important habitat, so it was also about educating people about our nesting birds,' says Holly.

Through the Plastic Free July initiative, Rottnest Island educates visiting students and holds regular beach clean-ups as a way of demonstrating plastic's negative impact on the environment.

'As an authority, we can only do so much,' Holly says, 'but the campaign has been great. It gives a platform for businesses to buy into it. There is momentum and a set of principles to help people respond. There's a lot of goodwill around Rottnest.'

Since the 2016 focus on plastic straws, Rottnest Island has made huge progress in its plastic reduction efforts. All businesses on the island support the Plastic Free July initiative and participate in efforts to reduce single-use plastic. The RIA itself does not use any single-use water bottles. Bench seats and boardwalk sections on walking trails are made from recycled plastics, and there are school holiday workshops in calico bag printing and recycled sculpture. Businesses now sell reusable cups and promote reusable bottles; some cafés reward visitors with a free coffee in return for a bucketful of beach rubbish.

Goodbye to plastic straws

Rottnest Island has a total ban on plastic straws, and paper straws are offered on request. The ban was developed in consultation with people with disabilities and representative organisations to ensure everyone's needs are met and alternatives offered.

Michelle Reynolds, executive director at the RIA, emphasised the importance of consulting with the business community. 'We worked really closely with the chamber of commerce on the island to achieve these results together,' Michelle says.

'Rottnest Island is such an inspiring place that people are willing to take that extra step to protect wildlife, such as the wedge-tailed shearwater, and preserve the unique environment. Businesses on the island are at the front line of our joint efforts to reduce plastic use and lead the community in turning the tide.'

Christine Parfitt was the waste engagement and education officer at the RIA at the time the ban was developed and introduced, and she emphasised the importance of consulting with the disability community.

'We held a focus-group discussion with some incredible people who required a straw in their daily lives,' Christine told me. 'It was fantastic speaking with these people and learning about their needs, many of whom had already switched to reusable straws because of their concerns for the environment. As a result of these discussions, each business was given a box containing a variety of straws to suit different needs. These straws are available to anyone who visits the island.'

•

Having conversations with participants and reading their stories is what I value the most during my daily involvement with Plastic Free July. It gives me hope that we can make a difference and provides inspiration for ways to grow the challenge and to help others act. Reading these stories is like going through a cherished photo album. Each time I go into this joyful labyrinth of discovery, it reignites my enthusiasm and belief that together we can make a difference. Yet I know that as long as there is a system where a material that will last forever continues to be used for just a few minutes and then thrown away, this story won't be finished. So here is one more that makes me smile.

In 2020, the first ever Bollywood movie to go plastic free on set, *Coolie No. 1*, is due to be released. Now *that's* something to sing and dance about!

9
We're all in this together

Perched on a bench outside my local supermarket in July 2018, I was there to see firsthand how my community was coping with the Western Australian government's ban on lightweight plastic bags. It was a sunny Saturday morning and this was day seven of the ban, so while people had already had some time to get used to the change, for many it would have been their first grocery shop where free single-use plastic shopping bags weren't automatically provided at the checkout.

Curious to see how people were managing, I sat with my notebook, alternating between reading, gazing into the distance, and surreptitiously checking out how they were transporting their groceries in this new single-use bag–free climate. I was also keeping a rough tally of people's choices. It was reassuring to see the general public carrying on with their grocery shopping, apparently unscathed. A silver-haired couple pushed their trolley with the groceries neatly packed into the supermarket's branded reusable bags, a young mum negotiated her way through the crowds with a calico bag hanging off the back of her pram, two friends in activewear carried a cardboard box packed with post-gym goodies, and a student sauntered along with a French baguette and a bunch of celery poking out of his backpack.

About a third of the customers simply cradled a couple of

essentials without the need for any bag at all. Previously, they would have emerged from the supermarket with just a loaf of bread or bottle of milk in a plastic bag – the formerly accepted norm. If something is given to you for free, why would you say no?

Yet if you had listened to popular media or followed the heated debate on social media, you might have thought that our modern lifestyles were under threat. How could we possibly go without something that had always been a given – and freely given, at that? Conversations on talkback radio were dominated by the adverse impacts and fears were fuelled. This wasn't just about inconvenience. Our health was at risk; our reusable bags were apparently hotbeds of bacteria and mould; our daily lives were about to be disrupted and businesses put in jeopardy. Such was the hype that you could have been forgiven for thinking a basic human right was being removed from our free and easy way of life. Some segments of the community were up in arms. What were the alternatives? How were we ever going to feed our families?

But watching the shoppers come and go outside my supermarket, I knew we were going to be okay. People would still be able to go shopping and the economy wasn't going to collapse. There were some teething problems as people took time to transition and get into new habits, and popular media had a field day turning those few glitches into sensationalised stories, but the majority of people just adapted and got on with it.

Not that I really thought that it would have been any other way. Even though it had been voluntary for me, once taking a free plastic bag was no longer an option I always remembered my own bags or managed without. It wasn't too hard. I had also been part of the project team working on the community education plan before the introduction of the plastic bag ban, and our research demonstrated strong community support for the ban. It also found the community needed reminders about the solutions, be that 'juggling' a few items, being a 'boxer' who recycled a box from the shop, going 'naked' with things loose in the trolley or simply doing the BYO bag thing. It was great to finally see it in action and the creative ways that people were coping. The ban only applied to 'lightweight' plastic bags (with a thickness of 35 microns or less) so sure, some had purchased the supermarket's 'reusable bags' that were made from thicker plastic, but these were in the minority. A large number of people realised they didn't need a bag at all.

I got a strong sense that the ban was going to make a difference. After all, though many people expressed concern about the plastic waste problem, as a community we were still using a lot of single-use plastic. While the ban might not have been perfect, it helped us to significantly change our habits; sometimes we just need a prompt or a reason to help us.

Across Australia I'd seen concern around plastic bags extend from individuals doing the right thing to community efforts such as Boomerang Bag initiatives, and individual local government authorities and businesses banning bags. Alongside this momentum, advocacy efforts through petitions and local government schemes ultimately resulted in the country's three major supermarket chains announcing they would stop supplying lightweight plastic bags on 1 July 2018. At the time of writing, New South Wales is the only state in Australia not to have introduced a ban. The public are concerned – so concerned that if businesses are seen to defy plastic reduction efforts, their actions are now widely denounced. Their social licence to operate is being challenged.

The power of collaborative action

There's an overwhelming sense of satisfaction watching people come together each year as a community to do the challenge and joining

> 'I knew Plastic Free July had become a powerful movement when I kept reading articles in the media about a supermarket's free plastic giveaways and the commentary questioning how the supermarket could do this during Plastic Free July – a time when so many Australians were trying to reduce their plastic waste.'
>
> – Dr Joanna Vince, political scientist, University of Tasmania

in as that momentum grows. It gives people a sense of meaning and belonging. Taking action together creates something bigger than any individual effort to the point where the challenge now feels like a phenomenon with a life force of its own. The power of Plastic Free July comes from not focusing on the problem but rather from offering people hope and choices to act on an issue of concern to many.

When I hear the question 'What difference can one person make?' I just have to reflect on the many stories I've been told over the years of people making meaningful changes beyond their own lives. It was only a few years ago in Western Australia that our then state government didn't support a plastic bag ban, but through the concerted efforts of citizens and community groups, eventually it was retailers that made the announcement – and now we have that state-wide ban. As the popular quote from Japanese poet Ryunosuke Satoro put it: 'Individually, we are one drop. Together, we are an ocean.'

Global campaigning for Plastic Free July

The same day the photo of the basket of cups from the Emu Point Cafe was spreading around the world on social media, my second coffee for the day was to have equally far-reaching effects. Later that day I had lunch with Colin Ashton-Graham, our behavioural economics adviser. We discussed the increase in Plastic Free July participation by organisations around the world, but we didn't really know the full extent of it. The previous year's general population survey in our home state had shown for every person who had signed up, there were another 63 people participating, and this was where it was close to home and had become fairly well known. If this was true for the rest of the world, we wondered, could we have more than 2 million participants across the globe?

In his usual measured and thoughtful way, Colin said, 'I might know someone who can help us with this.' Through Colin's introduction and a very generous pro bono offer, we commissioned the Melbourne office of global research company Ipsos to add Plastic Free July to their worldwide social survey. The aim was to find out how aware and engaged people around the world were regarding the Plastic Free July challenge.

Ipsos's survey in September 2018 revealed that 29 per cent of people surveyed in 26 countries around the world were aware of the Plastic Free July challenge and almost half of those had chosen to take part. I was flabbergasted. I would have been amazed if there had been 1 per cent awareness: we were such a tiny organisation, and we didn't even have an advertising budget. Using the Ipsos data combined with World Bank statistics showed that an estimated 120 million adults from 177 countries took part in Plastic Free July 2018. Plastic Free July had spread beyond anything we could have imagined and there were now many more people participating internationally than in Australia. It was an overwhelming statistic to try to get my head around. I thought back to that day in 2011 when I'd first decided to go plastic free for a month. I'd had nothing more than the determination to try it.

To me, the global reach of Plastic Free July was proof of the incremental power of small changes and grassroots action. It felt like a testament to all those people who had joined the challenge in their own way, and to the hundreds of groups and organisations around

THE HANDS LEAD THE HEAD

Colin Ashton-Graham

Behavioural economist

Reflecting back on the work we have done over the last couple of years to take Plastic Free July to a mainstream audience and help people to change their behaviour around plastic use, I have learned so much from working with Colin Ashton-Graham. I've been challenged to reconsider some of my assumptions – many that I didn't realise I had – which made me rethink some of my attitudes and the way we approach change-making.

When we did those original surveys that showed eight out of ten people were concerned about plastic waste ending up in landfill or the oceans, I couldn't quite believe it. How could so many people be concerned and still be using so much plastic? Maybe we just needed to provide better access to education about the problem and then everyone would change. After all, I kept being invited to speak and share my experiences of plastic pollution research expeditions, and I knew that people were really interested.

'You cannot easily guess what motivates a behaviour'
Colin explained these results in terms of an 'attitude–behaviour disconnect'. He pointed out just giving people more information wasn't the only answer. 'Let's challenge the assumption that awareness and concern *must* always be the first step, and that understanding is the sole driver of action,' he says.

Colin helped us to find out about people's behaviours, what motivates them and what 'gets in the way of a better behavioural choice'. When we went back to what was happening in the general community and asked questions like 'What are you doing?', 'What are your choices?' and 'What are you willing to change and why?', we were able to get to the crux of people's behaviours.

'The key thing is that you cannot easily guess what motivates a behaviour. That is why questions are more powerful than facts,' Colin says.

He offers an example of a project he worked on with residents living near an estuary. The project was to engage a gardening expert who would go into residents' homes and help them reduce their fertiliser use to improve the condition of the waterway.

'When confronting people with the problems with fertiliser use, they got one in 100 people – six people in total – to sign up,' he says. 'When we reframed the approach to ask *why* they lived near the estuary, things changed. People told us that they valued and wanted to help the waterway. Participation went up 25-fold. More than 100 people participated in the program.'

People *did* care about the environmental impacts of plastics, and so the solution was to help them to 'do the right thing', rather than telling them what they already knew about the problem. Simply reminding them to take their bags and to keep them in a handy place was more effective than confronting images of plastic pollution. The surveys and behavioural insights also helped us to figure out what to tackle for maximum effect.

'It is about solutions, not problems. If you ban plastic bags and tell people about environmental doom, they are left without a bag and feeling miserable. Instead Plastic Free July is about the amazing alternatives you have to the plastic bag, such as reusing a cardboard box or juggling a few items of shopping. When we offer a positive choice, the reason becomes secondary.'

– Colin Ashton-Graham

'The most promising behaviours are those that are already quite socially "normal",' Colin says. Avoiding pre-packaged fruit and vegetables is one example, although this is not always easy to do with current supermarket practices. Nevertheless, it is these kind of behaviours that encourage a significant proportion of the population to take up the action.

'Social surveys show us that people want to do what others do. Making change as a community and sharing stories can create new social norms and start to disrupt our culture of convenience. People increasingly see the "right behaviours", such as taking your own shopping bags, and the wrong ones start to disappear. It is what people *do* that leads the culture, which leads the behaviour of commerce and the policy of government.'

'There has to be some intrinsic benefit'

Colin attributes much of Plastic Free July's success to the way our campaign embodies 'best practice' in behaviour change. We look at what influences people, what engages people and how ideas spread.

'For any behaviour to stick there has to be some intrinsic benefit,' Colin explains. 'These benefits may be connection with people, joining a trend, personal satisfaction, taking control of meaningful choices or making a contribution to a better world. These are areas we don't always think about, but when you scratch the surface they are fundamental to almost all of us.'

He highlights the importance of the 'small ask'. 'With complex campaigns, for example those around climate change, the ask can become very big and it overwhelms our intellectual head space. As soon as something becomes uncomfortable, it can turn people towards denial or inaction – or opposite action … The less we have to struggle with intellectual and moral dilemmas, the less tired we are, and the more open to change.'

For Colin, one of the nicest things he sees about people embarking on Plastic Free July, and the intrinsic benefits of that journey, is that the changes are quite visible and accountable. 'The hands lead the head, not the other way around,' he says. 'In principle it is about keeping the ask small and keeping the reasoning secondary to the participation. So it is about the *doing*, not about the *why*.'

Offering choices also amplifies this positive approach. 'If there are ten things to change, let people just choose one for themselves. Offering choice offers control. If the ideas on the list include something that you are already doing, then you get immediate reward and a sense of contribution and connection.'

'There is nothing more miserable than a "fun fact". There is a sort of safety shutdown valve in your brain that just disconnects you.'

– Colin Ashton-Graham

A traditional campaign works on the principle of 'We know why and we are going to tell you.' Plastic Free July reverses that approach. Rather than tell you why and then tell you how, it is based on sharing the *how*, followed by an open question: 'How does it feel?'

Broadening the appeal

Offering choice was key, but it was also really important to reflect that choice in a way that appealed to all people. In 2019, updates to our branding and website reflected that. Even though we started the process by consulting a wide range of our participants, Colin pointed out that everyone we were talking to had already engaged with Plastic Free July and was already on the journey.

'Our target audience was actually the 90 per cent of people who were yet to do Plastic Free July,' he points out. 'We of course continued to support the pioneers and leaders who made this community, but our efforts were also now focused on balancing that with reaching out to the mainstream.'

the world sharing Plastic Free July in their communities. The research helped us to set the direction for our next steps and our communications. This really was a global campaign.

Reaching out to the mainstream

In 2019, we focused on the 90 per cent of people who were new to the plastic-free journey by coming up with six different representative 'personas'. It was a little bit like preparing for a screenplay;

having the characters helped us to know our audience. We gave each of these imagined characters a name and a full bio. 'Practical Pete' and 'Busy and Budget conscious Mary-Ann' were the two characters who represented the people yet to do Plastic Free July, while the other four characters described people who were already making efforts to reduce their plastic waste and who wanted support to take the challenge into their communities and workplaces.

This also assisted our approach to social media. We shared images of people from all walks of life with different options to reduce plastics in a range of settings, instead of the stereotyped perfection of a 'zero-waste' personality who would attract only a small segment of the population – and potentially disengage others. 'Practical Pete' probably wasn't going to respond to images of mason jars filled with lentils or even beeswax wraps, but it was almost guaranteed that he would care deeply about plastic litter at the park where he kicked a soccer ball with his kids, and he'd be more than happy to pack his shopping into a reusable bag.

Our most fundamental shift came from tailoring and testing messages with non-participants. People felt the 'Plastic Free' ask was too hard for them and at the same time perceived that only doing it in July would not be enough. The real ask became 'Choose to Refuse' (single-use plastics) as an embodiment of our established mantra to 'do what you can do'.

Behaviours usually shift slowly; the results shown on the next page from Plastic Free July 2019 represent a spectacular success in the world of behaviour change.

With Ipsos global surveys showing that 29 per cent of the global population are aware of Plastic Free July, and that 80 per cent of our global participants support policies and action to reduce plastic waste, it is clear that Plastic Free July is a significant part of a global change.

RESULTS FROM PLASTIC FREE JULY 2019 AROUND THE WORLD

- Participants reduced their waste and recycling at home by 23 kilograms per person for the year (i.e. by almost 5 per cent).
- Nine out of ten Plastic Free July participants made changes that have become habits/a way of life.
- They have a positive sense of wellbeing, which increases with participation in Plastic Free July.
- Participants are ahead of the global trends, being 16 per cent more likely to adopt plastic waste-avoidance behaviours.
- Unprecedented levels of media coverage – 2214 pieces reached over 100 million people in global readership.

Towards a circular economy

Whereas personal decisions such as keeping a set of reusables in the car can be implemented relatively easily and without huge preparation, there are many challenges to reducing plastic waste in our own lives that are beyond our control. These range from a lack of alternatives – such as supermarkets packaging produce in plastic, or the absence of bulk stores – through to limitations in waste services. People are also limited by their finances and their time. When I speak to people with busy lives, it's common to hear that groceries are ordered online, leading to a lack of choice in packaging or refill options. Not everyone has the luxury of a bulk store in their neighbourhood, so choices are sometimes constrained by what is on offer at the local supermarket.

Although food purchasing is the most commonly cited challenge for people trying to avoid single-use plastic, changes are definitely on the rise. Over the last ten years in Perth, for example, over a dozen bulk food stores designed to reduce waste have opened and there have also been localised changes in major supermarkets, such as less plastic packaging in the fruit and vegetable section, bulk dispensers and 'help yourself' unwrapped bakery products. The changes have often been implemented following consumer feedback; many shoppers want to support their supermarket and enjoy the convenience of being able to do their shopping in one place, but they also want to make plastic-free choices. Although these options are not yet available nationwide, retailers are definitely moving in the right direction. As consumers, we all help to drive those changes. It is important to help retailers to adapt their practices by choosing the unpackaged options that are available, offering suggestions and also providing positive feedback when those changes occur.

It was aboard the *Sea Dragon* in 2014 that I first started thinking about the role that individuals play and the need for change at a systems level. This seafaring journey was a practical experience of what it meant to have finite resources and I started learning about the need to move towards a circular economy.

> 'Circular economy thinking is all about keeping the product and its inherent value in the loop. A "circular" product is one that has been designed with the whole life cycle in mind. Products are designed so that the plastics are easy to dismantle and of a chemical composition that lends itself to recovery and reprocessing at the end of useful life.'
>
> – Dr Anne-Marie Bremner, waste management consultant

What is a circular economy?

In developed nations, making do with limited resources is something that many of us haven't experienced. Circumstances can change quickly, though. As bushfires destroyed whole communities in Australia at the start of 2020, it was sobering to see people lined up outside supermarkets to gain access to basic necessities. It brought to mind a different era. With large swathes of Australian land currently ravaged by drought, the luxury of infinite resources is no longer something we can take for granted.

When *Sea Dragon* sailed towards the Azores with our crew of 12, the food on board had been carefully planned to make the crossing. During my watch team's turn to cook, we had to check the meal plan and use only the ingredients allocated for that meal – we couldn't just duck out to the shops to get extra ingredients, and the packaging we did have was minimised as much as possible, as we had to keep it all on board with us.

It was an invigorating experience. Mission leader Kate Rawles would lead lively discussions and shared with us the story of Ellen MacArthur racing single-handedly around the world in 2001. Ellen's insights into what it meant to live with a finite supply of resources included hair-raising stories of repairs at sea in gale-force winds. She went on to establish the Ellen MacArthur Foundation, with the goal of shifting from our current linear economy to a circular and regenerative one. One of the key principles of the circular economy is keeping products and materials in use. 'Waste' is designed out of the system; the flow-on effect is that pollution is reduced.

Over the last ten years, Plastic Free July has given me the opportunity to explore and learn firsthand about some of the many initiatives to ensure plastic doesn't enter waste streams and add to pollution levels. Increasingly, legislation and regulations are being put in place to eliminate plastic, including bans on lightweight plastic bags and individual food serviceware items.

Spending two weeks in San Francisco during my Churchill Fellowship was a practical opportunity to see how the city's zero-waste-to-landfill goal and California's Trash Control Policy were being implemented. Visiting the famous Golden Gate Bridge wasn't on my itinerary; instead, I spent a rainy morning across the bay in Oakland looking into 'trash capture devices' in stormwater drains below busy city streets, and visiting facilities receiving waste from the City's mandatory recycling and composting services. It was a thought-provoking experience. I saw the challenges involved in getting the right material to end up in the right waste stream, and finding markets for end-product recycling. I learned about their policies to reduce rubbish and divert waste from landfill, including bans on plastic bags, polystyrene and non-recyclable food serviceware, a cigarette litter fee, and restrictions on the sale of bottled water.

In the city of Baltimore on the east coast of the US, rubbish that runs from streets and streams into the inner harbour is captured by a rather adorable wind- and water-powered 'trash wheel', complete with googly eyes. The current from Jones Falls River turns the waterwheel, which sets a conveyer belt in motion. Large booms contain floating trash and the rubbish is deposited into a bin that can be moved for emptying.

Jumping onto the small service boat and going out to 'meet' Mr Trash Wheel himself felt like an honour. It was quite mesmerising to stand on the pontoon and watch the waste slowly coming up the ramp before it dropped into the bin. It was autumn, so there were some leaves and branches in the mix, but the majority of what was captured was plastic. It was like seeing our throwaway society in slow motion; I couldn't help but think of the solutions. Water bottles could be tackled by people using their own bottles (eliminating waste through behaviour change), and more places could be offered to refill them (innovative solutions through better systems). A container deposit scheme would ensure litter was more likely to be

THREE STEPS TO STOPPING THE FLOW OF PLASTIC

According to the Ellen MacArthur Foundation, a 'New Plastics Economy' to address the problem of plastic waste at its source requires us to do three things:

- *Eliminate* all problematic and unnecessary plastic items.
- *Innovate* to ensure that the plastics we do need are reusable, recyclable or compostable.
- *Circulate* all the plastic items we use to keep them in the economy and out of the environment.

collected (circulating and keeping it in the economy and out of the environment).

Looking across to people standing on the waterfront with Mr Trash Wheel, taking photos and reading signs, I saw the celebrity factor at work. He is so popular he has his own social media account, but behind the scenes he is a serious type, having collected over 1200 US tons of rubbish in five years, and providing crucial data from rubbish audits to drive environmental policy changes.

Reuse initiatives

Container deposit schemes are a successful waste-reduction initiative with the bonus of offering financial encouragement for people to do the right thing. The schemes are a form of extended producer responsibility – beverage companies are charged a small fee to cover the collection and recycling of the containers – and the beverage containers collected through them are either reused or considered clean and thus have better recycling outcomes than mixed recycling. Paying a small amount for returned beverage containers has been shown to reduce beverage container litter by 40 per cent. It is yet another initiative that has been increasingly adopted by jurisdictions in Australia and internationally. Like the cans and bottles that are deposited, it really does feel like things are coming full circle – the idea seemed like a dream when we started advocating for it ten years ago.

Reuse initiatives link producers and retailers with a supportive customer base. On the South Island of New Zealand I spotted milk being sold in stores in returnable glass bottles and visited dairy farmer Andrew Moir of Windy Ridge Farm, curious to find out how the system worked. I'd known of a few companies using glass bottles but few actually collect the bottles for refilling. Andrew and his sons milk their 65 'girls', as he calls their cows, and then pasteurise and bottle the milk into one-litre glass bottles. They deliver a couple of times a week to retailers in the Otago region, where the milk bottles are quickly purchased by loyal local customers. On returning the empty cleaned bottles to their place of purchase, customers receive subsequent bottles for half the price and the Moirs collect these bottles at the time of delivery and return them to the farm. My visit to the farm coincided with the cleaning and sterilising of returned bottles, a labour-intensive process requiring specific equipment. Andrew confessed that after factoring in all the effort it would be cheaper for him to purchase new glass bottles, but he and his customers believe in the reuse system.

'The best thing I can remember is when I first started supplying milk, and was doing the deliveries to the few stores we had, all the customers would stop to tell me how nice the milk was, and it was just great being able to reuse bottles,' Andrew says. 'They think it is fantastic, and that made me feel so good!'

Reuse models that reduce the need for single-use plastics and put the responsibility back on businesses rather than customers are also on the rise. Individual cafés and towns have introduced voluntary reusable cup schemes, but initiatives can also come from a higher level, such as the 'Single Use Foodware and Litter Reduction Ordinance' introduced by the City of Berkeley in California. The ordinance requires food vendors that offer onsite dining to only use reusable foodware for customers eating on the premises, with a charge of 25 cents for every disposable cup provided. In Berkeley the company Vessel offers an exchange service for stainless steel reusable cups, a tech-enabled option for customers who haven't brought their own cup for a takeaway drink. There are a growing number of these reusable service models for businesses and events popping up around the world. The global 'circular shopping platform' known as Loop, created by TerraCycle in the US, is designed to eliminate the idea of waste. Customers order their favourite brands in reusable containers; these are home-delivered, with the packaging collected or returned to the store, creating a circular system.

Alternative packaging

It will take time to find solutions to the plastic waste problem, and a lot of innovation is still required, particularly in the transportation and packaging of food. It is not about simply substituting one form of packaging because of its environmental impacts with another material that will come with its own set of environmental impacts. Graphic designer Kate Lindsay – one of the original Plastic Free July participants, and the designer behind our turtle logo – works with fruit and vegetable growers, and knows some of the challenges they face in finding alternatives to plastic packaging.

'Growers are making great inroads and want to do the right thing and reduce plastic but finding a way to get products to the market loose and in a condition where they are undamaged and saleable has been difficult for small businesses,' Kate says.

'We'd love to have alternatives to single-use plastics that do the same job and are affordable,' says Doriana Mangili, business manager at the Sweeter Banana Cooperative in Western Australia, a cooperative of 25 growers who have a niche market by growing small 'lunch box' bananas. 'But at the moment there is no easy solution because our bananas have very thin, soft skins, so when they are loose during transport or overly handled, they mark and bruise very easily.'

I have been to a lot of waste facilities in my time. It is actually incredibly interesting. It's not just an activity for people in community programs such as Earth Carers; I think it's something we should all do. I often wonder what advances may have already taken place if everyone – from product designers, to business managers, and through to policy makers – visited their local waste facility as I did all those years ago.

When considering alternative packaging materials, we need to consider the end-of-life impacts if they end up as litter, as well as their fate in waste management facilities. There is much confusion around terms such as bioplastics, biodegradable, degradable and compostable, aided by misleading and unclear marketing claims. In a nutshell, we need to look at what they are made of, where they end up and how and what they break down into.

Taking a break from writing one day, I walked along the beach near Joanna's house and photographed the dog poo bags in the dispenser. 'We care for our environment,' the print exclaimed (along with a lovely picture of a dog doing its business under a tree). 'This bag will degrade after disposal.'

On another occasion, I retrieved a plastic bag on the footpath with the following message in an ocean-blue font: 'This is a 100% totally degradable and recyclable plastic bag. Please re-use this bag in the interest of the environment.'

These 'degradable' plastics are conventional plastics that include additives to break up more quickly when exposed to heat or UV

WHAT'S IN A NAME?

The United Nations Environment Programme (UNEP) report *Biodegradable Plastics and Marine Litter* provides useful information on these terms:

- *Bioplastic* refers to what an item is made from. Bioplastics are produced from biomass (organic matter), such as sugar cane pulp or cornstarch. This word doesn't tell you anything about what happens to the item if it ends up in the environment, or its recyclability.
- *Biodegradable* items will break down through biological processes (bacteria and fungi) to its component parts: water, CO_2/methane, energy and new biomass. The conditions under which it will biodegrade vary widely, e.g. it might require high temperatures that are only found in industrial composting facilities (50 degrees plus Celsius).
- *Compostable* items are capable of being broken down at elevated temperatures in soil under specified conditions and time periods. Again, this often requires the high temperatures found in industrial composting facilities
- *Degradable* or *oxodegradable* items fragment partially or completely into smaller pieces of plastic through UV radiation, oxygen or pro-oxidant additives that accelerate degradation.

radiation. This simply breaks up the problem into smaller pieces of plastic, yet I suspect the local authority had purchased these in good faith. Even certified biodegradable and compostable products often require processing in industrial composting systems where temperatures reach 50 degrees plus Celsius.

Over the years I have experimented with putting different materials and packaging types into my home compost and worm farm. The only thing that remained of a pair of cotton underpants in the worm farm was an outline from the synthetic elastic and stitching. Results from packaging have been more variable; I have found some tea bags and a supposedly compostable bag more or less intact a year later.

I discussed the role of bioplastics with CSIRO scientist Denise Hardesty. These are plastics made from renewable feed stocks, such as plant oils or cornstarch. Denise posed a logical question: 'Are we going to grow food for the world's people or are we going to grow crops for packaging?' she asked. 'Using bioplastics for everything is not going to work in the current system, but the solutions need to be viable in lots of places and in lots of environments.'

Ultimately the aim with all solutions is to work towards that circular economy, design out waste and pollution, and start to value our resources. In nature there is no such thing as waste. Relying on a linear system has reached the end of its shelf life.

Recycling in action

The mission of the Plastic Free Foundation is to dramatically reduce plastic use and increase recycling. After China's waste import ban and other countries following suit, recycling hit the headlines around the world – and deservedly so. It forced us to face up to our rubbish. Given that at that time the world was recycling just 9 per cent of our plastic waste, I think of it more as a wake-up call that has made us start to understand and discuss the complexities. Sure, there are challenges with our waste and recycling system that we need to address, but the solutions don't need to start there.

I was given my go-to shopping bag back in 2012, at a beach clean-up we organised in July, by local reusables company Onya.

This handy shopping bag stuffs into a neat pouch and despite being used almost daily and going everywhere with me since, it is showing no signs of wearing out. I joke that this is unfortunate as it's a dull grey colour and not as attractive as the brightly coloured bags with Australian prints that Onya makes today.

The company uses fabric made from recycled PET plastic bottles and now also supports the work of the Plastic Free Foundation. Although it isn't the cheapest method of producing the bags, managing director Hayley Clarke says it is by far the most eco-friendly.

'Virgin plastics are more accessible and are around four times cheaper, but when you weigh up the cost of recycled material versus virgin plastic (or even natural materials such as cotton) it actually has a far lower footprint in terms of CO_2 emissions and water use,' Hayley says.

The underpinning philosophy is all about 'turning off the tap of plastics'. 'I get asked why we don't make the bags from organic cotton, but apart from all the water used, we've got to solve the problem we have now. What do we do with the millions of tonnes of plastic we already have? We can't just ignore it.'

We discussed how important it was for businesses to use recycled content in products and packaging. In the EU, as part of their efforts to reduce plastic pollution, plastic bottles will have to contain 30 per cent recycled content by 2030. Having mandated recycled content would help support the recycling industry by providing markets for the end product.

'Businesses should be rewarded for [using] recycled materials, rather than being punished because it's more expensive. If we do recycle then we should also be buying recycled materials, otherwise our recycling becomes just stored waste.' Extending recycling from simply putting products in the recycling bin through to ensuring we purchase products made from recycled materials is part of the whole-picture solution, Hayley says.

A bigger environmental picture

On Earth Day 2019, the global market research and consulting firm Ipsos released results of a worldwide survey in which they had asked people which environmental issues were most concerning to citizens. Across the world, global warming/climate change, air pollution and dealing with the amount of waste we generate were the top three environmental concerns.

The rapid rise of waste as a major concern to people around the world surprised me, as did the way that plastic had become the poster child of environmental issues. The highly visible nature of plastic, its undeniable source and the devastating impacts on wildlife all combine to tell a compelling story that requires our action. Made from fossil fuels, produced in ever-increasing amounts for items that we often use just once, plastic embodies the overconsumption and excesses in our society.

How plastic waste fits in

At the time of writing much of this book, vast tracts of Australia's landscape were on fire. In the aftermath, the statistics were hard to fathom. Approximately 12.6 million hectares had been burned, devastating communities with the tragic loss of lives and homes and an estimated one billion animals. The scale of these fires was unprecedented and difficult to comprehend; they even created their own weather systems. Mass evacuations took place and a state of emergency was declared. The images of families huddled on beaches, children motoring their siblings and family pets out of harm's way in dinghies, and navy vessels shipping people to safety against the haze of an orange sky seemed surreal. This wasn't just a problem in the regional communities directly affected by fire. Smoke also filled major capital cities and offices closed due to health risks. In Sydney, Canberra and

Melbourne air pollution exceeded hazardous levels and respiratory masks became the new accessory on the streets.

Against this environmental devastation, plastic pollution was certainly not the most urgent problem, but it is a culturally crucial part of the bigger picture. Reducing plastic waste also has flow-on effects. Environmental issues like climate change, water pollution, the depletion of natural resources and overpackaging of consumer goods would all be addressed in part by decreasing our plastic consumption. For many people, reducing their plastic footprint is the first step to reducing their carbon footprint, and reducing their carbon footprint is a first step to advocating for more sustainable commerce and government. When we try to reduce waste, it makes us reconsider what we need, where the items we choose to buy have come from and what ultimately happens to them.

A really obvious example is avoiding food and other consumables wrapped in unnecessary plastic. Do we really need an individual peeled mandarin in a plastic box or six avocadoes in a plastic tray covered in plastic film wrap when the recipe only called for one? Buying local produce, or starting your own veggie and herb garden, not only results in fresher food, it also reduces the carbon emissions from freight, and reduces food packaging and storage costs. Less land clearing and deforestation for the production of biopackaging, fuels and cosmetics has positive effects for wildlife habitat and biodiversity. If the growing demand for palm oil used in food and cosmetic products (often packaged in plastics) is stemmed, it will cut back on tropical deforestation. Less plastic means less air pollution from plastic production, from the manufacture and transportation of goods, and from the disposal of those goods. Ironically, as the world begins to make a shift away from fossil fuels as a source of energy, large oil companies are investing heavily in new petrochemical plants to ramp up plastic production, and this too will greatly increase greenhouse gas emissions.

BEING PART OF THE BIGGER PICTURE

- Start with the hands and share the 'how'. Make a change yourself, then share with your friends, family or wider community how you did it.
- Buy less.
- Choose products made from recycled content.
- Repair what you have and make things last.
- Value food and the people who grow it.
- If your favourite brand or product comes in plastic, give them direct feedback about your concerns (customers can influence change).
- Care enough about environmental issues to make it drive the way you vote. Invite your local MP or mayor to do the challenge.
- Celebrate the positives. Support initiatives and businesses with a circular approach by highlighting their achievements, not just shortcomings or failures.

A whole emerging area of concern and increasing research is the human health impacts of plastic. This goes beyond plastics within our food, such as plastic that has been found in seafood, salt and honey. It is in the air we breathe and, disturbingly, research is emerging that shows chemicals in plastic packaging are contaminating our food and putting our health and the health of future generations at risk.

If this all sounds a bit overwhelming, it can be summed up very simply. It reminds me a bit of that common question, 'How do I lose weight?' For most people who do not suffer from a specific medical condition, there is a very simple answer: eat less, move more. In terms of plastic and the flow-on effects to our environment, using less *always* results in less harm.

Food waste

Globally, by weight, around one-third of all the food we produce each year goes to waste. In countries such as Australia and the US, it is more like 40 per cent. To put this in perspective, if food loss and waste were its own country, it would be the world's third-largest carbon emitter – surpassed only by China and the US. As well as the financial cost of wasted food, there is an environmental cost: when it ends up in landfill it releases methane, a powerful greenhouse gas contributing to climate change. When food produced for our consumption goes to waste we also waste water, energy, land, fertiliser, packaging and other precious resources.

In my home, reducing plastic packaging on the food we buy has also reduced our food waste and food bill. By buying in bulk and as locally grown as possible, planning meals and using what we already have, and eating leftovers and composting food scraps, we now have very little food waste, though my children would argue that I sometimes have been a little too creative in my use of leftovers. Our family gold-star food waste award probably still has to go to my granny, who once put leftover salad in a soup. It resembled an oil slick, complete with floating wilted brown lettuce leaves. Even I couldn't eat it.

There is an argument that plastic packaging of produce can reduce food waste through keeping food fresh for longer. Eating food when it's fresh and just buying what we need can reduce this. It is a trap going into a store to buy a couple of carrots only to discover it's 'cheaper' to buy a whole bag. Not only do we end up with plastic, but often we waste food. When supermarkets offer a reduced price for purchasing two perishable items when we only need one, it feeds into that same thought process. There is always a risk of the rest going to waste, particularly if the items are on sale because they are near the end of their shelf life.

Of course it's not always as simple as saying no to all packaging. Some fragile items such as berries require sturdier containers.

Our European participants in Plastic Free July have shared photos of berries packaged in paper-based punnets, but when these options aren't available, of course the best approach is to do what you can with what is available in your area, or choose alternative fruits that don't pose this dilemma. The humble orange, for example, is perfectly packaged by nature.

Properly exploring all the issues around the merits and impacts of production and disposal of different packaging materials is a complex task. Needless to say the solutions aren't just as simple as substituting plastic for another material and at this point in time we don't have all the solutions. There is much scope for new research and innovation at all levels. The plastics problem has evolved over 100 years and we can't expect to solve it overnight. To paraphrase Michael Pollan, in his book *In Defense of Food*, 'Eat (real unpackaged) food. Not too much (just buy what you need). Mostly plants (grown as close by as possible).'

Governments get involved

In March 2020, Australia's Minister for the Environment Sussan Ley hosted the first ever National Plastics Summit at Parliament House in Canberra, attended by senior stakeholders from industry, government and community sectors. 'Everybody is onboard and everybody wants to be part of the solution,' Minister Ley said in her opening address. Standing in the queue chatting to the Western Australian Minister for Environment, Stephen Dawson, and Tim Youe from the recycling facility where I'd had my penny-drop moment, I marvelled at how far we'd come for the plastics issue to be taking centre stage in our national parliament, with leaders from multinational companies making pledges on how they will help to address the plastic challenge.

Over recent years we've started seeing Plastic Free July changing what we do all the way to the top. Not only in relation to the waste hierarchy (by focusing efforts on the reduce message) but also from champions of change in all levels of government and by politicians of all political persuasions. It is a positive campaign that offers practical solutions to an issue of concern to people around the world; it can be done by individuals and within an organisation as well as being 'shareable' with any audience (clients, customers or community).

I'm delighted when I see government representatives overseas advocating to increase awareness and action in response to the challenge of plastic pollution. Last year Australian high commissioners in Canada and Kenya challenged each other to participate, the British Embassy in Kyrgyzstan and the German Embassy in New Zealand shared a commitment to Plastic Free July on social media, and the US Embassy in Cambodia has previously held a community screening of the film *A Plastic Ocean*.

In 2018, former Canadian environment minister Catherine McKenna and MP Julie Dabrusin took part, sharing with their constituents, and challenging all members of parliament to participate and highlight the work of initiatives in their communities. The following year Canada's Prime Minister Justin Trudeau announced that certain 'harmful' single-use plastics would be banned such as plastic water bottles, bags, cutlery and straws. 'We owe it to our kids to keep our communities clean – and that means keeping them free from plastic waste,' tweeted Prime Minister Trudeau on 31 December 2019.

Though the plastic bag is often the first common item to be tackled through regulations, increasingly lawmakers are taking steps to address other problematic single-use plastics. In 2019, the European Parliament voted to ban a sweeping array of single-use plastic items as part of a new law against plastic waste. As well as targeting the most common plastic items littering beaches, this directive also includes single-use polystyrene cups and those made from oxodegradable materials. In January 2020, China went a step beyond banning plastic waste imports and announced moves to phase out single-use plastics through restrictions on the production, sale and use of items.

Michaelle Solages is a member of the New York State Assembly who found Plastic Free July online while searching for solutions not long after we built the original website. She has been doing the challenge ever since. Apart from taking action in her own life, as a legislator she has worked to introduce a number of laws to tackle single-use plastics and encouraged her colleagues at the Assembly and the New York State Department of Environmental Conservation to participate and share the challenge in the state of New York. Michaelle helped to introduce a plastic bag ban in New York State – where over 23 billion plastic bags are typically used each year. It came into effect on 1 March 2020. Having a conversation with Michaelle gave me a glimpse into how the challenge ripples out from the personal to a wider sphere of influence and across the globe.

In the New York State Assembly, 2019 was the fourth year Governor Andrew Cuomo passed a resolution declaring July as Plastic Free July in the state of New York (Assembly Resolution No. 586, 17 June 2019). The resolution highlighted that New York residents could take part in the initiative by 'giving up single-use plastics for a day, a week, or the whole month' during Plastic Free July, reasserting our message that any person from any place can take part in whatever capacity they are able to.

'Plastic Free July continues to accentuate the importance of being green and continuing to reduce the amount of plastic we use in our lives,' the resolution stated. 'In recognition of the great accomplishments of the Plastic Free July Initiative, an educational and reaffirming month-long challenge is held across New York State.'

Australian senator and former economist Peter Whish-Wilson has been campaigning to remove plastics from the oceans for almost

> 'If you had said to me five years ago that an initiative like Plastic Free July could make a difference, I probably would have been very, very sceptical ... but now I totally understand as I've watched it unfold that unless you have that action at an individual level, you are never going to get those changes in parliament and at a systemic level. It's like you can make change once you have taken action yourself.'
>
> – Peter Whish-Wilson, Senator for Tasmania

14 years, so he was surprised at just how 'bloody difficult it is to live without plastic' when he participated in Plastic Free July. 'It really didn't hit home for me how difficult it is to do without plastic and also how much plastic we use until I did the challenge,' Peter says.

Peter reinforced the power of many people acting together. 'We need systemic change and for that we need millions of people making change at the same time to be really effective. People feel empowered when they take action, especially individual action, and it becomes a tangible issue.'

Asked what the future looks like, Peter is adamant about a set of solutions encouraged through strong leadership. 'I'd like to see Australia have a reputation globally for leadership. We are a country surrounded by ocean; no matter what your political persuasion is, no one wants to see pollution in our oceans. We need to stop more going in and then we've got a job on our hands to clean up what's already there.'

Governments have a big role to play in regulating the use of plastics, he says. 'We need a full suite of national product stewardship schemes, full regulated bans of stuff we don't need, and governments need to properly fund tackling this issue ... I want people [in the future] to be saying to me, "I can't believe you used that stuff, that you needed to wrap bananas in two layers of plastic."'

What I've observed in the change makers and leaders working on this issue is their personal efforts to be part of the solution. I'm convinced this is where change has to start. I love seeing the Western Australian Minister for Environment, Stephen Dawson, with his stainless-steel water bottle at events, and hearing how New York's Michaelle Solages started by doing Plastic Free July personally. On social media I saw a picture posted by Peter Whish-Wilson of him holding a ceramic bowl at a café counter with the words:

> Yesterday, after just one week, I nearly broke my Plastic Free July pledge when I forgot to bring a take-away container with me. Luckily they let me go back to the office and get this bowl. It really is amazing to see so many businesses accepting BYO containers ... thanks to groups like Plastic Free Launceston who have converted many local businesses! It makes the Plastic Free July challenge much more achievable.

•

Thinking about the bigger picture for a sustainable planet, I can see how many people taking small actions such as by doing Plastic Free July is a powerful force for change. Governments are introducing regulations in response to growing community concerns, resulting in the spread of sustainability measures and greater validation for those already making a difference.

10

Life beyond plastic

I can't fully explain or begin to understand how a spontaneous idea that led to a grassroots campaign started by 40 people in Perth in 2011 grew to reach an estimated 250 million people worldwide by 2019 – all without an advertising budget. As Colin Ashton-Graham says, 'Plastic Free July is a story of what happens when people do things … and then others come along and join in … and surprising things happen.' In our team we sometimes refer to it as the 'magic of Plastic Free July'.

From a young age I've felt keenly the impacts humans can have on the environment. I couldn't *see* the rising salt in the landscape and river that forced our family to leave our farm, but I could certainly *feel* the impact it had on us. Being confronted by my waste on that visit to the recycling facility was the start of a journey exploring plastic waste around the world and, more importantly, learning more about the people and ideas that contribute to the solutions.

The problems are real and the numbers can be overwhelming. I can no more imagine the 8 million tonnes of plastic entering the world's oceans annually than I can the number of people taking part in Plastic Free July. What I *can* see is that my weekly shopping now has a lot less plastic in it, and I know that every piece I can avoid is one less piece that will be left behind, and probably outlive me, somewhere in the environment. And I can see others around the world doing their bit too – and they are all just ordinary people.

When I think about making a difference, I don't think of 250 million people; I think of Vandana in India reducing the plastic her food is packaged in despite sometimes having to buy bottled water, or Cynda and Laura from Margaret River making Boomerang Bags, or Nick having a laugh with his football team in Auckland by putting a $2 fine on plastic tape. I think about Anne-Marie taking her containers to the local butcher in an English village and Jackie getting cafés in Santa Cruz to put their plastic straws away. I reflect on the people who took on the challenge of reducing single-use plastic in their own lives, and then took the next step and shared it more widely.

Personal benefits

In 2019, Plastic Free July participants together avoided 825 million kilograms of plastic waste, including millions of single-use drink bottles, coffee cups, packaging, straws and plastic bags.

Wherever I go in the world I meet people who take part in the challenge and make a difference. I always feel a connection, even though our experiences and situations may be very different and the reasons for making change vary.

In San Francisco, an impromptu Plastic Free July picnic really brought this home to me; it was organised by Anne Marie Bonneau, who writes the blog *Zero-Waste Chef*, and the Bay Area Zero Waste Meetup group. A lively group of friends old and new turned up on a sultry summer's day to share stories of how we came to adopt this way of living. The picnic was a communal array of homemade dips and salad, bread, cheese, fresh fruit and spiced nuts, all brought in jars and metal containers and shared among the group. Everyone had brought their own reusable plates and cutlery. As we ate I enjoyed listening to people's stories of their journey and what had brought them to the park that day.

Kathrin Spoek grew up in Austria living what she describes as a low-waste lifestyle, but in later years fell into the single-use waste trap through convenience. Since deciding to reduce her waste several years ago, she's come a long way but admits she isn't perfect. 'My husband and I still do not live a zero waste life, but we create much less waste than before and we are more mindful about all of our purchases.'

As a registered dietician, Kathrin believes a plastic-free lifestyle not only contributes to a cleaner planet but it offers people personal health benefits.

'Packaged foods make it easy to consume a large volume of calories, salt, and unhealthy fats and may thus contribute to obesity and other issues,' Kathrin said. 'Transitioning to a plastic-free lifestyle limits the availability of calorically dense, processed food. Readily available package-free foods will often be limited to fruit and vegetables. Although some bulk stores will sell sweets and snack foods, the majority of bulk foods require preparation and are often rich in fibre and other beneficial nutrients.'

Rachael Edinger came with her husband John and nine-year-old daughter Maggie to the picnic. She brought picnic supplies using Maggie's bento box.

Maggie said that the lunches sold at her school had a lot of plastic packaging, but some kids were now using lunch boxes, and some children had asked for lunch boxes just like hers. 'I like it. I'm a little bit different from everybody, but I'm not very different,' she told me.

The whole family brainstorms ideas and alternatives to reduce their single-use plastic and break habits. 'There's a lot of "secret plastic" in things you wouldn't think are plastic and we do the research,' John said.

Rachael had known about Plastic Free July for years. She grew up on a farm in Washington state and her family ran a home-based bulk food cooperative. As an adult, deciding to avoid plastics didn't happen until after her daughter was born but was a return to the values she'd grown up with.

'I wasn't going to let my kid live in plastic or sleep in plastic or put plastic in her mouth or feed her with it. I didn't do it for my own health but I did it for her.'

Anne Marie Bonneau has been promoting Plastic Free July to the Bay Area community for years. She went plastic free in 2011 after reading about plastic swirling in the ocean. 'I said to my daughter, "We have to get off this stuff. I don't want anything to do with it. I don't want to be a part of this."'

'Once you start, you go down a rabbit hole and you can't stop. There are so many benefits and it is so much fun.' She told me that she's the healthiest she's ever been in her life.

Reimagining our food system

As I write this chapter, I'm taking a break in my state's south-west near the small city of Albany, sitting at the table in a holiday cottage I've rented for a week while my youngest son and his cousins are on holiday. They are exploring while I write. I'm distracted by the turquoise water and contrasting iridescent white sand of the bay. Even more than the view, I'm distracted by the salt grinder on the table, left there from last night. My thoughts drift back to our meal's accompanying conversation. The owners had thoughtfully left a small array of pantry staples including a transparent salt grinder containing crystals of 'Pink Himalayan Salt'. On closer inspection, the packaging was a plastic container with a cap made from a harder type of plastic but the grinder mechanism was fixed – refilling with rock salt didn't appear to be an option. This durable grinder was intended to be a disposable item. My nephew read out the fine print on the label: 'Packed in South Africa with ingredients from Pakistan'.

Himalayan salt from Pakistan, packed in South Africa. That took a while to sink in. Eventually, I gave in to the distraction and did some Googling. I located the supermarket's website and found out that the salt grinder cost a mere $3. Yes, a bit more expensive than regular table salt but when I thought about all that packaging and then the journey from Pakistan to South Africa (and sometimes Italy or China) and finally to Australia, I was dumbfounded and more than a little annoyed. I discovered that the salt's main source was the Khewra Salt Mine in the Punjab region of Pakistan. I wondered about how this mine operated, the conditions of the workers employed there and their salaries.

I also thought about our salt grinder at home, a functional and sturdy metal object with a refill chute on the side and a handle on top to grind coarse salt to the desired texture. It was a durable lifetime purchase (actually a gift from my husband) which will outlast me and no doubt be passed down to future generations. Since that first Plastic Free July, I have been buying salt from my local bulk food store. I started out purchasing 'Celtic sea salt', somewhat seduced by the name as well as the light-grey tint that made it seem healthier. My focus when doing this was solely about reducing plastics, but then I switched to Australian rock salt to reduce my food miles. Now I purchase salt that is sustainably harvested by a three-generation-strong family business from a salt lake about 400 kilometres from my home. Thinking back to our ecological footprint and Earth Overshoot Day, it seems unconscionable that we would transport salt halfway around the world to package it in salt grinders that we throw away after only weeks or months of use where they will be forever laid to rest in landfill.

The issues we've discussed in this book are not just about plastics. Plastic is more of a symptom of the much broader problems we have around our footprint being too large and the subsequent impacts on our environment.

> 'Many New Zealanders, including many children, write to me about plastic – concerned with its proliferation over the last decade and the mounting waste ending up in our oceans.'
>
> – Jacinda Ardern, New Zealand Prime Minister, 8 December 2019

One of the early Plastic Free July participants, Erin Rhoads, reflected on the sometimes difficult journey of change and what that has meant to her. She says we can point fingers at corporations and governments, but at some point we have to admit that it's partly our fault. 'The easiest change is yourself as opposed to changing politics or business, but at the end of the day, they follow our trends.'

For Erin, changing what we decide to buy is crucial. 'Our actions are important, not just our votes.'

It's also really important to distinguish between the incredible innovations that plastic has enabled and the unnecessary waste a throwaway society creates. It's the purpose, not the material, that's the issue. 'In the context of a prosthetic limb or a cochlear implant, plastic is a wonderful material,' Erin says. 'It's what we've done with it that's the problem.'

Erin's vision for the future looks back to the past for answers. 'I would like all my food to be grown closer so there is no need for plastic, and to see the takeaway culture of food and drinks reduced. We've lived without wasteful takeaway packaging for thousands of years,' she says. Erin is pragmatic about the need for some food to be transported, but questions the need for 'frivolous food', a term she uses to describe food that's a want rather than a need, such as grapes grown overseas so we can eat them in winter, or fancy cheese made on the other side of the world. Apart from the carbon impact of transport, she feels strongly about supporting local growers and producers, especially when many farmers and small businesses are

WHY SHOULD WE REDUCE PLASTIC?

Here's what our future generations from Australia and beyond have to say.

- 'Because sharks and ducks and frogs will eat it and it makes them sick. Plastic isn't good for the environment!' – Jasper, 3, Australia
- 'My teacher said a bad man threw rubbish in the sea and a whale ate it and died.' – Thomas, 4, United Kingdom
- 'It affects your health, your society, because when you throw rubbish in the lake or river and then when it flows down past people and they use the water then they get sick.' – Srey Leap, 11, Cambodia
- 'To stop the rubbish mountains from growing so much.' – Michaela, 4, Australia
- 'Plastic destroys the world and there is too much of it!' – Louis, 9, Australia
- 'This is plastic. Plastic is bad for the Earth.' – Te Ariki, 3, New Zealand
- 'Please think of the small children in your life, and what will happen to the oceans many years from now if we don't act now. We won't have a clean beach to play on because the ocean will be full of plastic!' – Ada, 7, and Antawn, 10, United Arab Emirates
- 'The reason I think plastic is bad is because it can kill millions of animals and we use oil to power plastic production which is bad for the environment ... The other reason I think plastic is bad is because it takes an extremely long time to biodegrade. The government is not taking enough action and this is serious.' – Joseph, 9, United Kingdom
- 'It affects the water and can kill the fish in the water because it pollutes the water ... it turns the water from clean water to dirty water.' – Leak, 8, Cambodia
- 'So it doesn't pollute the earth.' – Ivy, 8, Australia
- 'Because it kills planet Earth and if planet Earth is not clean, we will get sick and disappear.' – Skyla, 6, Canada
- 'Plastic is bad. Plastic harms animals, birds, water, plants, fish, flowers.' – Prisha, 3, India
- 'So that future generations can live in a safe world that isn't polluted by rubbish. Animals will have homes that are clean.' – Emma, 13, Australia
- 'So fish populations don't die off forever.' – Samion, 13, United States

doing it tough. She worries about how farmers feel when, as a country, Australia wastes nearly half of the food that is grown.

'I want people to question and never stop questioning,' she says. 'Who is growing my food? Are they paid well? How is their mental health? I don't want to assume the system is okay. I'd like to see more community gardens and more hubs for people to come together and learn new skills ... If we really looked at our food system and changed that, the impacts could spread out quickly.'

Future generations

When I ask people why they take part in Plastic Free July, a common response is that they want to leave the world a better place for their children.

It is difficult to hear the concerns from young people – they are so aware of the problem. We can have conversations with them about the problem but the most important thing is what we *do*. Our actions speak louder than our words. I remember coming home tired late one afternoon and wanting to buy something for dinner. Parked outside the fish market, I asked my youngest son Ronan if he would mind going in, and handed him our reusable container. He must have been about nine or ten at the time, and when he came out I asked if he felt embarrassed or uncomfortable asking to be served in his own container. He looked at me quizzically and replied, 'No, why would I?'

As the mother of a young son, Erin Rhoads thinks we need to start changing our language. 'We don't use the words "garbage", "rubbish" or "trash bin" in our house. I make a conscious effort to rephrase what is rubbish to help set up foundations that will enable him to see potential in everything. When food is left uneaten he'll say "Save for later", "I eat later" or "Use again". Usually it's me eating it or he'll help me take the food scraps to the compost to feed the worms and bugs. If a toy is broken he'll automatically ask for it to be fixed,' Erin says.

Imagining a cleaner future

I've asked a lot of people working on the issue to imagine what a future without plastic waste would look like to them, so I'll share what it looks like to me. One day I want to walk along the shoreline at my local beach and look down at shells and seaweed, and not be expecting to find plastic. I want to be able to look up and out at the horizon and not wonder if the ship coming into the harbour is carrying a cargo load of stuff we don't really need or that we'll just use once, and be confident that the ship sailing out of the harbour isn't full of our waste for someone else to deal with. To me, this would mean that I was living in a community where we'd shifted to doing the right thing and were living more lightly on the Earth. For Joanna, the future involves the simple pleasure of walking along the pathway to her local beach without the need to take a bag to collect plastic rubbish. It is also a future where she can look her children in the eye and say that our elected representatives are doing everything they can to protect and preserve the environment.

We have spoken to a range of people, from oceanographers to football coaches, and have considered their hopes for the future in relation to a broader world view – the discussions went so much further and deeper than clean beaches. In many cases, reducing plastic was the initiator of further change, a tangible way to make a difference, a springboard for other social and environmental initiatives, and a starting point for thinking about how all these issues intertwine.

Healthy communities

Some discussed plastic pollution in relation to the health and education of their communities. Nyikina man Victor Hunter, founder and director of the Foundation for Indigenous Sustainable Health (FISH), firmly believes that we need to keep educating people about the role plastic plays in diet and wellbeing.

Victor's vision for the future is 'a community without plastic from wrappings, containers and bags and an educational program that makes the connection between the creation of a healthy environment for people to live in, and the good health of the people themselves'.

Māori woman and general manager of zero waste initiative Para Kore in New Zealand, Jacqui Forbes, sees a future where food is produced locally and where processed and packaged foods are reduced. This, she says, will deliver changes to community diets, relationships and a sense of connectedness.

'For me, what success looks like is local food production, and I guess just healthier diets. When I fast forward, the dream I have for Māori is that there's orchards and there's food growing everywhere. That kai (food) can be harvested locally from rivers, streams, the ocean, harbours and the bush. Māori and non-Māori aren't separated and living in different spaces,' she says. 'It will lead to healthier people and happier people … and stronger resilient communities, so people actually self-determine in their communities.'

For Jacqui, plastic is really a symptom of a much greater problem and the focus should be on 'designing out waste'. 'Why would you buy unhealthy, processed food when you could have a nectarine with wrinkly skin that has been sweetened on a fruit tree by Tama-nui-te-rā (the sun)?' she asks. 'Real food is sweeter and better than anything that you could ever get in a supermarket.'

Scientists' vision

As the person responsible for the viral video of a turtle in visible pain as a straw was pulled from its nose, I was curious to know what marine biologist Dr Christine Figgener's vision for the future was.

'First of all, it would be that I stop seeing my sea turtles suffer and die from plastics, be it because of entanglements or ingestion,' Christine says. 'For me, it would mean I would be able to go out and eat without having a bad conscience, because I don't need to stress out about each unnecessary plastic item I might have been otherwise able to avoid. Lastly, it would likely mean we would see a general improvement in the health of a lot of people, because we are only now discovering how detrimental plastic and the toxins on and from plastics are for human health.'

Oceanographer Dr Julia Reisser also sees plastic reduction's alignment to broader environmental approaches, particularly climate change.'It's not that we should stop talking about plastic, but maybe we should use it as a flagship for the climate change problem, which at the end of the day is the same problem,' she points out, 'to really tell people the issue here is that we're relying on fossil fuels and not giving fossil fuels the value they deserve.'

Our oceans are just part of the picture, she says. 'Currently our target is to stop the flow of plastic to oceans and I think perhaps that shouldn't be the target. It should really be about bringing circularity to the materials.'

'We need to look at the problem more holistically,' she adds. 'What about the implications of plastic pollution to economies and human health?'

CSIRO scientist Denise Hardesty says we will know when we've done our job when 'our stormwater drains aren't full of trash' and when 'we don't see people littering cigarette butts or anything else'.

'We'll know we've done a good job when there's been a substantial cultural shift. That's not to say that we're not going to continue to use plastics, but that we're going to use them smarter and better, and reuse them and recycle them, and we're going to make thoughtful long-term design with intent for circularity decisions around some of this stuff.'

Denise knows more than most the devastating effect of plastic on marine animals, and that the path ahead, despite our advances, is a long one. 'We'll know we've done a good job when we see fewer animals with plastic in them. Although, given the current rate of plastic production, we've still got an avalanche or a sea of trash behind us and being produced every day. Even as we move towards zero waste lost, it's not going to disappear from our environment overnight. It's just not.'

We need to value the materials we use and produce, Denise says, so that materials are 'recovered and reused and reproduced', at the same time redesigning what we make and reducing waste 'all the way up and down the supply chain'. And, like others working on a daily basis with the outfall of mass plastic production, Denise calls on corporates, governments and individuals to show leadership and act sustainably.

Drivers of change

As the founder of a sustainability consultancy, Nick Morrison's vision is for a world where renewables are embraced, and innovative materials and systems that function in harmony with the real world will

> 'I think we will know we've resolved this issue when we've put a proper price on plastic that takes into account the cost and consequences, and we don't view it as a cheap and easy material.'
>
> – Dr Denise Hardesty, CSIRO research scientist

> 'I think we have fulfilled our very important role and now we need to make sure our next strategic exertion of pressure is in the right place – to get politicians and corporates to do their bit.'
>
> – Tim Silverwood, co-founder, Take 3 For The Sea

mean that our throwaway mindset is eliminated. 'We will live in a world where plastic is made entirely from renewable sources and the power to manufacture, transport and process it will all be renewable,' he says.

'All packaging will be certified compostable or infinitely recyclable. There will be deposit schemes in place on all packaging items, with networks of community return depots ensuring they make it to the composters or recyclers and creating meaningful jobs in those communities. Single-use plastics will only be used where absolutely required (e.g. medical purposes) and our streets, beaches and waterways will be entirely free of plastic pollution.'

Support for innovation and leadership also drives Take 3 For The Sea's Tim Silverwood. 'What fuels me to keep going with my activism is to put Australia on the map as a world leader to protect our oceans from human impacts. Community participation and community projects are one thing, but the action being taken at a political and corporate level maybe doesn't match up with the community appetite,' Tim says.

Tim's future vision is one where policy makers and business leaders step up and support the progress that's been successfully driven by community leaders.

'I can reflect back to my blind naivety in thinking it wouldn't take much to convince politicians and corporates to ban the bag, or to put the 10-cent refund [for drink containers] in place. I realise now that in politics and big business they are experts in gauging what the popular perspective is, and so you really do need to build the community fabric to a point where it becomes unavoidable,' he says.

For some, the future may mean that efficiencies take their skills in new directions. Waste manager Gunther Hoppe says the challenge now and for future generations is to create a process where we use materials wisely, and design products and systems to encourage a circular system instead of the take-make-throw culture.

Success for Gunther could mean looking for a new job. 'Although we run a commercial landfill, our mission statement is all about winning back waste. It's all about reducing landfill. The more effective we get at achieving our mission statement, the less waste there will be. We are actually working ourselves out of business,' he says.

For early adopter of Plastic Free July and waste management professional Dr Anne-Marie Bremner, the future recognises the value of plastic in the mix of solutions. 'It seems most likely that rather than eliminating plastic, we will value it,' Anne-Marie says. 'In the future, plastic will no longer be the cheap, ubiquitous product it is now. Rather, plastic of the future would be valued for the amazing product it is … [but] used in a circular process, constantly recovering and regenerating materials we need.'

'It will be interesting to see if there is a shift away from storing food in plastic or giving children plastic toys as the research into the human health impacts progresses,' she adds. 'Reclaiming our lives away from convenience all sounds a bit "zen" and improbable right now, but change is clearly needed and given the changes we have seen even in our own lifetimes, you never know what is possible.'

•

When I reflect on the last ten years and my journey into the plastics issue, I find my mind wandering back to those days on my childhood farm and how much the environment gave me, but also my awakening to its fragility. We are thankfully becoming aware of the impact of plastics and the legacy of our throwaway society. Change takes time, and yet in this relatively short time I have seen the cumulative impact of individual actions and how they merge and build momentum more powerful than any one of us. Plastic is symptomatic of the bigger challenges facing our environment that we need to address. This story has given me hope that our individual efforts and our stories matter. A lot of people doing one small thing is more important than just a few people trying to do everything.

In the words of anthropologist Margaret Mead, 'Never doubt that a small group of thoughtful, committed, organised citizens can change the world; indeed, it is the only thing that ever has.'

Postscript

> Humankind is now facing a global crisis ... When choosing between alternatives, we should ask ourselves not only how to overcome the immediate threat, but also what kind of world we will inhabit once the storm passes.
>
> – Yuval Noah Harari, *Financial Times*, 20 March 2020

On Monday 6 April 2020, I woke to Queen Elizabeth's voice on the radio as she spoke to the United Kingdom and Commonwealth in only her fifth such address during a 68-year reign. 'While we have faced challenges before, this one is different. This time we join with all nations across the globe in a common endeavour, using the great advances of science and our instinctive compassion to heal,' she said. Her rallying call-to-action was in response to the COVID-19 virus – a respiratory disease first identified in Wuhan, China, that had spread to become a global pandemic.

The Queen's speech was exactly one month to the day that Joanna and I had finished copy-editing this book. We breathed a sigh of relief at the time, but that was short-lived as we watched events unfold. In early March, the coronavirus was making headlines around the world, but for Australians the impact was largely discussed in relation to an unfathomable shortage of toilet paper. In the laconic style Aussies are admired for, much was made of the toilet paper rush, but under the surface, the sense of uncertainty, even fear, was palpable. This became more obvious as each day brought new social distancing rules and restrictions, and ever-changing modelling statistics of the virus spread. After the World Health Organization declared the disease a pandemic on 11 March, non-essential gatherings of more than 500 were cancelled in Australia and people arriving from overseas were forced to self-isolate. My home state of Western Australia declared a state of emergency.

Although changes were taking place almost daily, some things stayed the same. At the start of our third week of social isolation, my morning walk at South Beach was as beautiful as ever, but my response to what was happening around me was different. A littered takeaway coffee cup lid on the ground presented a dilemma. Should I pick it up? Who had used it? On the horizon, Rottnest Island was visible beyond the cruise ships with nowhere to berth. Instead of my usual associations with Rottnest – relaxing holidays, the delightful quokkas, stunning scenery, and the island's efforts at plastic reduction – I was instead thinking about the passengers who had disembarked on an island now being used for quarantine.

My local café and restaurants were closed. You could still buy a takeaway coffee, but most places were no longer accepting reusables. There was less traffic on the roads and more people seemed to be walking and riding bikes. Next door, the children started chalking the footpath with colourful pictures.

Work became a new frontier too. It was not just trying to home-school and work productively. My son Leeuwin returned from Sydney and we quarantined him for two weeks. As Joanna and I held Zoom meetings, I joked that the shadowy figure behind me was my escaped hostage. Joanna's daughter Chloe was negotiating a whole new way of learning in preparation for her Higher School Certificate. She lost the casual job she'd held for three years – those pillars of independence and certainty were crumbling in different ways for each of us. We all had to be more adaptable. Preparing for a webinar with behavioural economist Colin Ashton-Graham, I was jittery about whether the technology would work since our plans to run the webinar from our new office had to be abandoned while we hunkered down at home.

Of course, the direction of Plastic Free July was at the forefront of my mind. I'd already called Colin to discuss whether we should go ahead with Plastic Free July in 2020 at all. Would it be better playing it safe and not run it this year, or change it to Plastic Free November? Obviously, health considerations overrode any other concerns and with so many people experiencing financial hardship, food item shortages and store closures, avoiding plastic was going to be a greater challenge than ever before. Colin had a different view. He thought that Plastic Free July could 'give people the opportunity to do something positive'.

When we finally started the webinar, local councils who had taken up a new membership package with the Plastic Free Foundation had understandable questions:

- Will the 'choose to refuse' single-use plastics message be a harder sell after the COVID-19 crisis?
- Will this [essential at the moment] germ phobia be a habit that will be impossible to break?
- Can we ever go back to reusables?

Colin's words were encouraging (as much to me as to our audience). The challenge was going to be different – but by focusing on positive actions and what people *could* do, we could support our participants and fill a need.

'It's a really valuable thing we are offering because right now much of the distress comes from people feeling like the world is out of control, and that can lead to anxiety and depression. Doing meaningful things, in your home, for Plastic Free July can be an antidote to that,' Colin says.

'There is a lot of doubt and worry and the response to that has been a run on seedlings ... there's been a run on flour and sugar. People are not home baking to avoid plastic wrap on a commercially bought cake. The drive is to be more self-sufficient and to do something productive. We can see that the need for Plastic Free July is, if anything, greater than before as something that helps people with solutions relevant to being at home.'

•

I'd certainly seen many examples of people being positive by making small changes and doing what they could. Before my usual visit to the farmers' market, I had emailed my order in advance and stallholders Chris and Charlie had pre-packed my fruit and veggies into a crate so we could then fill our bags. The coffee van was open but only selling takeaways and you couldn't stop to chat with friends, so we bought a bag of locally roasted coffee beans to have at home. I bought a sack of flour from my local bakery and did my bulk shopping online. It was packaged in paper bags and delivered to my door.

As a family, we were trying more than ever to support small, local businesses, and the responses from others via social media reinforced the fact that many others were doing the same. When I shared a photo of some bread I'd baked and asked the community if they'd found their reducing plastic packaging skills handy during the coronavirus crisis, there was an immediate response from people around the world sharing their ideas and recipes and sending mouth-watering photos from homemade muffins, flatbread and scones, through to pasta, apple cider vinegar and tortilla chips. Many shared stories of creative ways they were using up their pantry supplies, revisiting old favourites, or trying new recipes.

Plastic Free July participant Wendy described how the skills she had developed were more invaluable than ever. 'I think people that have been active in plastic reduction seem to be managing a lot better. They're used to adapting and using creativity to navigate problems that arise,' Wendy says.

Replying to online comments and sharing recipes took me back to the early days of Plastic Free July. It was the same buzz, when everything was new. We didn't know the answers to every question, but we shared ideas and learned as a community. We were in this together.

•

Naturally, there's a concern that the response to COVID-19 will threaten the progress we've made in reducing single-use plastics. Across the world many food businesses have recently stopped using customers' reusable cups for takeaway drinks and some states and countries have banned the use of reusables including shopping bags.

People are worried about a continued acceptance of reusables after the virus passes and a perceived danger in terms of food purchasing and hygiene. Will the current fear that reusables could transmit the virus or other diseases be impossible to overturn?

I spoke to Professor Mary-Louise McLaws, Professor of Epidemiology, Healthcare Infection and Infectious Diseases Control at the University of New South Wales and adviser to the World Health Organization, and her expertise was reassuring.

'The most important things we can do to avoid the virus are hand hygiene (hand washing) and social distancing. There is this thought that we must have very sophisticated models to understand good infection control and outbreak management, and that the development of vaccines is the solution to focus on. We can't lose perspective on the importance of the simple solutions [for control of this and other epidemics], including washing our hands and cleaning high touch surfaces. We need to be using soap and water or sanitisers with over 65 per cent alcohol content, wiping over reusable shopping bags and washing reusable coffee cups.

'This idea that we somehow need to go back to using disposables – the coronavirus is just not an excuse. As to cafés not accepting reusable cups; it fails logic. As long as baristas are practising good hand hygiene (which they should be doing anyway), are regularly washing their hands and not touching the rim of the cups then they should still be used.

'It is really sad to think we aren't taking care of Mother Earth at this time; it's not good enough. We can do two things at once – take care of our health *and* reduce our impact on the environment. There is simply no excuse,' Mary-Louise says.

In a *Huffington Post* article on 7 March 2020, Pittsburgh-based Dr Amesh Adalja, a fellow of the Infectious Diseases Society of America, has a similar view. 'Minimizing exposure should focus on washing hands, not eliminating the use of a reusable water bottle at work. I don't think that people's office water bottles are going to be the way that this pandemic unfolds. It's coughs and sneezes ... but there are people that are worried about the most esoteric means of transmission, and I think that kind of detracts from the main message here, that this is a respiratory virus: Wash your hands, don't touch your face, cover your coughs.'

The advice I have read about risks from fresh produce is similarly comforting. In an article by CSIRO scientist Cathy Moir, she concludes 'It's not a gastrointestinal virus. The acid in our stomach is expected to inactivate the virus. There is no evidence to suggest you become infected from eating coronavirus. The best advice is to wash your hands with soap when preparing fruit and vegetables and to rinse fresh produce with water just before you eat it.'

•

None of us know the long-term impacts of COVID-19, how long we need to adhere to social distancing, or when we will return to 'normal' work practices, leisure activities and living arrangements. Meanwhile, Plastic Free July has allowed me to connect with people all around the world, and I've often thought about our extended plastic-free community and how people are coping with their unique circumstances during the pandemic. My concern for Michaelle Solages and her community in New York eased when I viewed her online, working at a food distribution centre. I read that in South Australia, sustainable packaging company Detmold Group behind the Detpak brand has employed extra staff to manufacture millions of surgical and respirator masks to help stop the spread of the coronavirus.

I also heard from Vandana K, reporting on the impact of the coronavirus lockdown from the streets of New Delhi and how her workload has increased because journalists are frontline workers.

'I've had to kind of let go of some of the aspects of my zero-waste lifestyle in the last two weeks – half of my groceries still come without packaging but everything else is packed. I cannot compost either as my composting unit is in a public park (a few minutes from my home) where I donate my compost. Under the lockdown, I can't go there.

'I've had to employ a waste worker, giving him both wet and dry waste a few times a week. I also pay him extra because I know he's a frontliner too and very vulnerable at a time like this.'

Scott Brannigan, co-owner and chef at Bread in Common restaurant in Fremantle has had to close his new venue just two weeks after opening. The business has adapted, selling boxes of fresh fruit, vegetables, bread and preserves to the local community. At his small distillery he makes gin and a few alcoholic liqueurs for restaurants using waste bread and offcuts that he ferments and turns into alcohol. With the advent of the coronavirus and the shortage of hand sanitiser, he has started making his own to use in the kitchen. He also supplies the mother of one of his staff to help keep her acupuncture business open.

'My focus has been on the garden and keeping the soil cultivated so we are ready to produce when we open again,' Scott says. 'We are also doing things for the community such as opening the kitchen once a week to cook pre-made meals for food charity OzHarvest.

'We want to give a little back when times are tough ... they don't have enough food to distribute with all the restaurant closures. I'm looking at it as a bit of a restart: there are definitely things we can do better when we open again, including managing our waste and reducing our environmental impact. We need to have purpose in these times,' Scott says.

Businesses that have responded to the community's ever-growing desire to reduce plastic are hopeful that the aftermath of the pandemic will ultimately be positive. Although many premises are no longer accepting reusable cups for takeaway beverages, their long-term environmental outlook remains optimistic.

'These times can be uncertain and challenging but they remind us that we're part of a global community, that together can, and will, overcome this,' Abigail Forsyth, co-founder and managing director of KeepCup says. 'The COVID-19 pandemic clearly shows us how we can effectively drive change when we band together. The climate and plastic pollution crises will still be here when we return our focus from fighting the immediate threat of coronavirus. Let's not trade one crisis for another.'

Author of *Zero Waste Home*, Bea Johnson, spoke about the need for resilience and hope in an ever-changing landscape.

> I can't predict the future and know what it holds for bulk [produce], especially with mandates currently changing constantly from one store, city, or state to the next, but what I do know is that the zero-waste lifestyle makes us resilient, self-sufficient and therefore highly adaptable to change. It is one of the greatest advantages that I have discovered about this way of life.

> 'Human health is, of course, the ultimate priority, but the environment, and Plastic Free July's work, is also integral to human health.
>
> Dan Dragovic, Partner Herbert Smith Freehills.

•

When Joanna and I embarked on this book, we both recognised there would be highs and lows, and we made a pact that we wouldn't 'go down at the same time'. As long as one of us was in a positive and reassuring state of mind, that was all we needed to keep going. We somehow managed to maintain that status quo, but of course neither of us could have predicted what would unfold.

After a particularly challenging week for me, we chatted on the phone. The far-reaching impacts of the virus were becoming real. The Western Australian container deposit scheme had just been deferred, with Environment Minister Stephen Dawson saying 'there are too many potential health risks and logistical difficulties to start the scheme in June 2020'. Joanna and I had both been reading through the final manuscript of this book and individually pondering the relevance of every chapter, every sentence, in a landscape that was changing every day. With such a critical health and economic crisis affecting people around the world, could this still be the inspiring story it had been just a few short weeks earlier? I thought it could, though maybe in ways that I hadn't anticipated. Joanna thought so too:

> What your story has shown me, what this book will convey, seems even more relevant now. I mean, here we are working from home and home schooling and 'Zooming' and dealing with partners or friends who've lost their main source of income and taking on unanticipated challenges every day *and* baking. That's a lot of change and it can feel overwhelming. You can't take all that

on at once, but that isn't the message of this book. The Plastic Free July message is about taking small steps and supporting each other. It's not about beating ourselves up when we've had a bad day or when things feel completely out of control.

There are many things I can't be sure of at the moment, but what I do know is that I'm still able to keep doing what I can with what I have, and appreciate the small daily victories. Staying at home is challenging, it has restricted our freedom. We miss family and friends more than ever, but those still able to leave their homes for exercise have been able to get to know their neighbourhood better. There are so many stories of people's creativity and the way they are caring for others in the community. I hope this global crisis gives us a moment to pause and think about what it is we really need. With stores closed and shopping limited to essentials, the current situation has certainly been a disruption to our throwaway society and culture of convenience. It has flowed through to disruptions in supply chains. The expectation of being able to buy any product during any season is not feasible at the moment, and perhaps simplifying our expectations and buying food grown locally is one of the positive things to come out of these very difficult times.

The combined efforts of every one of us to flatten the coronavirus curve gives me hope that we can also start to flatten the curve of exponentially increasing plastic production. No one has been able to ignore the remarkable effect that restrictions placed on travel and industrial activity during the pandemic has had on the environment – significant and rapid changes including clearer skies, cleaner rivers and even wildlife appearing on city streets. Like many, being confined at home makes me more fully appreciate the strong link between our communities and the environment and how intrinsic they are to each other.

Taking responsibility for our actions is more important than ever.

Resources

Plastic Free July: plasticfreejuly.org

Non-profits and community organisations

Algalita Marine Research and Education: algalita.org
Earth Overshoot Day: overshootday.org
Green Music Australia: greenmusic.org.au
Para Kore: parakore.maori.nz
Plastic Soup Foundation: plasticsoupfoundation.org
Say HI to Sustainability: sayhitosustainability.com
Tangaroa Blue: tangaroablue.org
The Ocean Cleanup: theoceancleanup.com

Campaigns and projects

Bags Not: bagsnot.org.nz
Beat the Microbead: beatthemicrobead.org
Boomerang Bags: boomerangbags.org
Break Free From Plastic: breakfreefromplastic.org
BYOBottle: byobottle.org
Green Music Australia: greenmusic.org.au
International Coastal Cleanup: oceanconservancy.org/trash-free-seas/international-coastal-cleanup/
Responsible Cafes: responsiblecafes.org
ReThink Disposable: rethinkdisposable.org
Take 3 For The Sea: take3.org
The Last Plastic Straw: thelastplasticstraw.org
Plastic Pollution Coalition: plasticpollutioncoalition.org
Two Hands Project: facebook.com/twohandsproject/

Books

Susan Freinkel, *Plastic: A toxic love story*, Melbourne: Text Publishing, 2011
Bea Johnson, *Zero Waste Home: The Ultimate Guide to Simplifying Your Life by Reducing Your Waste*, New York: Scribner 2013
Kathryn Kellogg, *101 Ways to Go Zero Waste*, New York: Countryman Press, 2019
Lindsay Miles, *Less Stuff*, Melbourne: Hardie Grant, 2019
Charles Moore with Cassandra Phillips, *Plastic Ocean*, New York: Avery Books, 2011

Michael Pollan, *In Defense of Food: An eater's manifesto*, London: Penguin, 2010
Erin Rhoads, *Waste Not*, Melbourne: Hardie Grant, 2018
—— *Waste Not Everyday*, Melbourne: Hardie Grant, 2019
Beth Terry, *Plastic Free: How I kicked the plastic habit and how you can too*, New York: Skyhorse, 2015

TV and film

Bag It (film): bagitmovie.com
Blue Planet II (series): bbcearth.com/blueplanet2/
A Plastic Ocean (film): aplasticocean.movie
'Plastic Oceans', *Catalyst* (TV episode), abc.net.au/catalyst/plastic-oceans/11013966
The Story of Stuff (short film), storyofstuff.org/movies/story-of-stuff/
War on Waste (series): abc.net.au/ourfocus/waronwaste/

Blogs and online resources

Eco With Em by Emily Ehlers: ecowithem.com
Gippsland Unwrapped by Tammy Logan: gippslandunwrapped.com
Going Zero Waste by Kathryn Kellogg: goingzerowaste.com
'Plastic detox: Deplastify your life' by Jane Genovese: learningfundamentals.com.au/go-plastic-free-find-your-strength/
The Rogue Ginger by Erin Rhoads: therogueginger.com
Treading My Own Path by Lindsay Miles: treadingmyownpath.com
Zero-Waste Chef by Anne Marie Bonneau: zerowastechef.com
Zero Waste Home by Bea Johnson: zerowastehome.com
—— Bulk Finder App: app.zerowastehome.com

Education and training

Living Smart courses: livingsmart.org.au
NSW Environment Protection Authority (EPA), *The Story of Waste: Community Engagement Advisor training manual*, Sydney: NSW EPA, 2019, epa.nsw.gov.au

Research and reports

CSIRO, *Marine Debris Research*, research.csiro.au/marinedebris/
Roland Geyer, Jenna R Jambeck and Kara Lavender Law, 'Production, use, and fate of all plastics ever made', *Science Advances*, vol. 3, no. 7, 2017, e1700782, advances.sciencemag.org/content/3/7/e1700782
Ipsos, *Earth Day 2019: How does the world perceive our changing environment?*, Paris: Ipsos, 2019, ipsos.com
Jenna Jambeck, Roland Geyer, Chris Wilcox, Theodore Siegler, Miriam Perryman, Anthony Andrady, Ramani Narayan, Kara Lavender Law, 'Plastic waste inputs from land into the ocean', *Science*, vol. 347, no. 6223, 2015, pp. 768–771,
Peter John Kershaw, *Biodegradable Plastics and Marine Litter: Misconceptions, concerns and impacts on marine environments*, Nairobi: United Nations Environment Programme (UNEP), 2015, wedocs.unep.org/handle/20.500.11822/7468
Tammy Logan, 'What the law says about using your reusable containers', *Gippsland Unwrapped*, 18 August 2016, gippslandunwrapped.com/2016/08/18/the-law-using-reusable-containers/

Ansje Lohr, Heidi Savelli, Raoul Beunen, Marco Kalz, Ad Ragas and Frank Van Belleghem, 'Solutions for global marine litter pollution', *Current Opinion in Environmental Sustainability*, vol. 28, 2017, pp. 90–99

PlasticsEurope: Plastics – the Facts 2013 (2013)

PlasticsEurope, Plastics – the Facts 2015 (2015)

Plastics – the Facts 2019 (2019)

Qamar Schuyler, Britta Denise Hardesty, TJ Lawson, Kimberley Opie and Chris Wilcox, 'Economic incentives reduce plastic inputs to the ocean', *Marine Policy*, vol. 96, October 2018, pp. 250-255 https://www.sciencedirect.com/science/article/pii/S0308597X17305377

United Nations Environment Programme (UNEP), *Legal Limits on Single-Use Plastics and Microplastics: A global review of national laws and regulations*, Nairobi: UNEP, 5 December 2018, unenvironment.org/resources/report/legal-limits-single-use-plastics-and-microplastics

United Nations Food and Agriculture Organization (FAO), *Food Wastage Footprint: Impacts on natural resources – summary report*, Rome: FAO, 2013, fao.org/3/i3347e/i3347e.pdf

Anna Maria van Eijk et al., 'Menstrual cup use, leakage, acceptability, safety, and availability: A systematic review and meta-analysis', *The Lancet Public Health*, vol. 4, no. 8, 2019, PE376–E393

Chris Wilcox, N Mallos, GH Leonard, A Rodriguez and BD Hardesty, 'Using expert elicitation to estimate the impacts of plastic pollution on marine wildlife', *Marine Policy*, vol. 65, April 2015, pp.107-114.

Chris Wilcox, Erik van Sebille and Britta Denise Hardesty, 'The threat of plastic pollution to seabirds is global, pervasive and increasing', Proceedings of the National Academy of Sciences, August 2015, 112(38), pp.11899–11904

World Economic Forum and The Ellen MacArthur Foundation, *The New Plastics Economy: Rethinking the future of plastics*, Isle of Wight, UK: Ellen MacArthur Foundation, 2016, ellenmacarthurfoundation.org

Acknowledgments

Thank you to Elspeth Menzies from NewSouth Publishing who contacted Rebecca after her own plastic penny-drop moment. Without your belief that this was a story worth telling, the book would not have come to fruition. Thanks to the wonderful staff at NewSouth Publishing, particularly Emma Hutchinson, Harriet McInerney, Joumana Awad and Rosie Marson for going above and beyond in your support for us and your own efforts to reduce plastic, even through the production process of this book. Thanks, also, to Emma Driver for your copy editing expertise, humour, patience and dedication to shaping the story, and Josh Durham for his enticing cover design.

This book is about many people with many stories to tell. Thank you to all those who have shared their experiences and trusted us to tell them; we are eternally grateful. We especially thank Colin Ashton-Graham for so generously sharing his knowledge and insights into change-making and for helping to shape this book to inspire people.

Many people have supported us in practical ways that helped to get words on the page, particularly our families. To Jo's parents Vicki and David – your hospitality and the tranquil writing refuge was a great boost to our creativity.

It is not possible to acknowledge everyone, but we would like to thank all those who have taken on the Plastic Free July challenge. I have only had the opportunity to meet a small number of you, but without you there wouldn't be a movement or a story to tell.

Rebecca Prince-Ruiz

Jeremy, thank you for your support and belief in me and this project I've become so passionate about (some may say obsessed) over the last ten years and for holding our home and family together while I went off to write with Joanna. To Pepita, Leeuwin and Ronan (and Tiller), your love for nature inspires me to act. Thanks for enduring my absences and putting up with all the changes in our household to go 'plastic free'.

Plastic Free July would never have become a movement without my dream team colleagues – Amy, Nabilla, Gabrielle and Bec and the Earth Carers; it was the ideas and enthusiasm from this group that made it happen. Thanks to Shani and Tim who started me off on this sustainability journey, 'Living Smartie' Alex H, whose war on plastic in 2009 planted a seed, and the Winston Churchill Trust for your generous fellowship. To my board, advisers, volunteers and the Plastic Free July team, thank you for your personal commitment and your dedication. Thanks to my father, Carlos; my mothers Jean and Leigh; my siblings Kelly, Kate and Adi; mentors Jennifer and Horst, my 'wise women'; and all those whose support and friendship has made this journey possible.

And to Joanna, thank you for saying yes when I asked you to write this book with me. I knew I needed someone who could see into the stories of the movement and tell them in an authentic way. Having binge-read your beautiful book *Watermark* and hearing about your own Plastic Free July journey I thought you would be the perfect person to ask. After reading the first words you wrote for the book, tears came to my eyes because you could describe the story I wanted to share so beautifully that I knew I was right. Thanks for your enthusiasm and patience through all the ups and downs and for the sacrifices you made to write with me. Without you this story could never have been told.

Joanna Atherfold Finn

The first time Rebecca came to my home, I was completely paranoid about plastic. Our household had improved a lot, but as a family we were far from perfect. I felt as though I was seeing everything through her eyes. As we worked, my dog sat under the dining table gnawing on a plastic toy that squeaked plaintively. I offered Rebecca a cup of tea to deflect attention from the plastic mauler at our feet.

'Jo, you probably don't want me to tell you what many tea bags are made of,' she said.

No, I probably didn't. But I did learn about tea bags, and microbeads, and challenges around biodegradable definitions and some of the ways of dealing with them. I also learned that Plastic Free July is not about perfection. It's about doing what you can with what you have. There's no judgment, but there are many solutions. We can all learn a lot from that approach – not only towards plastic but towards any measures that aim to help, and not harm, each other and the environment we share.

Thank you to my family – Greg, Troy, Chloe, Sam (and Tilly) – your patience and ongoing belief helps me to keep writing every day, as does the serene haven we call home and the surrounding bushland that I can escape to when I'm lost for words.

To my parents, Vicki and David, and my sister, Kristy, thank you for your humour and unwavering support. Thanks, also, to my writing friends and mentors who inspire and motivate me, and the Plastic Free Port Stephens group who are spreading the plastic-free message in my hometown.

A special thanks also to my agent, Fiona Inglis from Curtis Brown, for your reassurance and encouragement.

Finally, thank you, Rebecca, for contacting me with the idea of collaborating on a book about Plastic Free July. I have not only had the pleasure of co-writing this publication, I have learned so much and made a true friend. Your quiet determination, positivity and authenticity are traits that make a great co-author. Those same qualities have enabled you to take the seed of an idea and nurture it into a movement that has inspired millions of people. It has been an honour to work with you on this story.

•

We acknowledge our carbon footprint while writing the book. As we live on opposite sides of the country we spent hours on the phone and much of the time it was a virtual writing process and our words floated together on the 'cloud'. For the travel we did take, we kept a tally and offset our greenhouse gas emissions through the Gold Standard Australian native reforestation project Yarra Yarra Biodiversity Corridor, in Western Australia.

Index

Index

INDEX

Index

About the Authors

REBECCA PRINCE-RUIZ is the founder of Plastic Free July. An experienced environmental management and sustainability professional, she speaks internationally about how to achieve a world without plastic waste.

JOANNA ATHERFOLD FINN is the author of the short story collection *Watermark* (2018). She is a freelance journalist and has taught at the University of Newcastle.